THE WORKS OF ANATOLE FRANCE
IN AN ENGLISH TRANSLATION
EDITED BY THE LATE FREDERIC
CHAPMAN AND BY J. LEWIS MAY

THE BRIDE OF CORINTH
AND OTHER POEMS & PLAYS

THE BRIDE OF CORINTH
AND OTHER POEMS & PLAYS
BY ANATOLE FRANCE
A TRANSLATION BY
WILFRID JACKSON
& EMILIE JACKSON

LONDON : JOHN LANE, THE BODLEY HEAD
NEW YORK : JOHN LANE COMPANY : MCMXX

TO
FREDERIC PLESSIS

ὦ τύμβος ὦ νυμφεῖον.
SOPHOCLES, *Antigone*

PREFACE

IN this book I touch on high matters, and delicate to handle; on religious matters. I have dreamed again the dream of the ages of faith; I have illuded myself with lively belief. To have treated what is pious with impiety would have been to lack the sense of harmony. I bring a sincere respect to bear on matters sacred.

I know that there is no certainty outside science. But I know also that the worth of scientific truth lies in the methods of its discovery, and that these methods are not to be arrived at by the common run of mankind. It is hardly scientific to hold that science may one day replace religion. So long as man sucks milk of woman, so long will he be consecrated in the temple, and initiated in some sort in divine mystery. He will dream. And what matter if the dream be false, so it be beautiful ? Is it not man's destiny to be steeped in perpetual illusion ? Indeed, is not such illusion the very condition of Life ?

A. F.

O MAIDEN HELLAS, young, with lyre in hand,
   Innocent child with kissed and honeyed mouth,
   Whose smile gave back the greeting of thy land,
The sparkle of the sea and sky and south,

Thy days and hours sped by on even feet,
And when dark night had silvered all the ways,
Thou, well content, cicalas shrilling sweet,
Wouldst brood upon mankind its works and days.

Child of the sea, on tawny beaches prone,
Thy breast voluptuous in beauty swelled,
What waves of harmony, of sacred tone,
Filled thee, and through thy song in fountain welled!

I, child of Latin race, who found thee fair,
And fed mine eyes, to do thy beauty praise
And paint thy goddess shape with faithful care,
Have done what time shall but in part erase.

Others have limned thee in thy tranquil morn
When, from the fountain whence thy gods would start,
Thou camest, bearing high the earthen urn.
Such peace may find no place in my sad heart.

Thy breast bear these pale violets for the dead.
I paint thee, Hellas, when a jealous god,
Tearing the sacred fillets from thine head,
Thee, in thy broken temple, bruised and trod.

Then the smile faded and the heavens frowned;
And grace and beauty perished with thy fall;
None raised thy lyre from off the stony ground,
And earth rolled on its course in gloom and thrall.

O daughter of the Graces, thee I sing!
Loved to the last, and fair all things above,
That they who read my verses' offering,
May hold life dearer and be kind to Love.

PERSONAGES

A Fisherman.
Hippias.
Daphne.
Kallista.
Phrygia, *the slave*.
Theognis.
Hermas.
Daphne's Nurse.
A Wise Woman.
Artemis.
Aphrodite.

Chorus of Youths.
Chorus of Vine-dressers.
Chorus of Christians.

THE BRIDE OF CORINTH

PART I.

A road between Corinth and the sea. Looking eastward and ringed with myrtles, a little temple, bearing on its entablature among fair mutilated shapes the monogram of Jesus, roughly cut. A fountain. Beyond, on the hillside, the coloured wal's of a house and an orchard. Vines. The Acropolis of Corinth show white on the horizon. It is evening: the sun is low in a quiet sky. OLPIS, *the old fisherman, sets down his baskets, and seats himself on a mound.*

SCENE I.

FISHERMAN.

FROM town to sea the road is long to tread,
    Fatigue soon met. And bitter is his bread
    Whose want town-hucksters to their greed subdue.
Fish in these days run smaller and are few.
No more they weight my basket and my net

Whence the sea-harvest, now but seldom met,
Poured in my favoured bark abundant spoil.
No more the gods assist a life of toil.
Behold, this very day, is all my catch
To wives of Corinth, and their cooks to match,
For thirteen wretched obols all transferred.
Grasping is woman, yet prodigal of word,
Bad are the times and men ; the gods retrace
Their steps from earth and an unworthy race.

Scene II.

The Fisherman, Hippias.

  Hippias (*he wears the Thessalian head-dress; his grey tunic is girdled round his loins; his high sandals are knotted about the ankles with leathern thongs. He has a white staff in his hand; and walks quickly*).
Hail, House and Grove, and maid beside the hearth
Spinning, who draw'st for me a sainted breath !
Say, Fisher (for thy baskets show wet sheen
Of sea-spume on their reeds, and sea-weed green)
Sure thou dost know it—this was Hermas' door,
Old Hermas—Say——

    Fisherman.
      He lives, my son, to store
In jars of ancient mould a this-year's wine—

THE BRIDE OF CORINTH

HIPPIAS.
The gods shed peace upon his fruitful vine!
Hast seen his daughter, Daphne, in her ways?
Is her life sweet, and do her youthful days
Pass on light wing nor touch her candid brow?

FISHERMAN.
The gods, who made her fair, love her, I trow.
She walks with modesty for crown and veil,
And she is happy—
        HIPPIAS.
           Friend, your news I hail.
Kallista then, to speak of her remains—

FISHERMAN.
She has stirred gods to wrath and now complains.
Unwise it were for one of lowly sort
To tell the curious news of grave import.
Certain it is, Apollo, as of old,
Against the wicked shoots his darts of gold.
                    [*He departs.*
HIPPIAS.
Yes, it is Daphne there, dazzling as snow,
Bending to gather herbs the path below!
Her neck, her bosom, more wonderful to sight
Than their importunate vision in the night.
I see her, long desired, and at her view
Falters my gaze with shock of something new.
The gods, who set her on my path to find,
Have touched her with a charm beyond our kind.

SCENE III.

HIPPIAS *and* DAPHNE.

DAPHNE (*before the temple*).
I gather dittany, of sovereign power,
And many a soothing herb in stalk and flower.
May I distil for her who gave me breath
A potent draught against the threatened death.
Christ, heavenly bearer of the healing word,
If other gods disperse when thou art heard,
And if Apollo man no longer hears,
Jesus, soft King, whose eyes are filled with tears,
God who hast suffered—surely Thy reign brings
Hope of a God to end our sufferings!
O Master, save!—My mother, too, is thine—
And bring to me the spouse they me assign.

HIPPIAS.
Daphne, dear wonder, all delight that is,
One is now come to fold thy life in his.
The promised spouse by custom of the race—
Behold, arise, and meet his wide embrace!

DAPHNE.
Yes, it is thou—no wraith that walks by day
To tell loved Hippias is cast away.
I knew, O wandering keeper of my heart,

THE BRIDE OF CORINTH

The days must end which kept us twain apart.
The hope was constant in my breast, nor fled.
Come, I will lead thee in where, with bowed head,
My mother weaves her wool: there, at her knees,
Recount, dear guest, the perils of the seas.
A sickness bows her, and consumes her veins.

Hippias.
Our days are mixed of pleasures and of pains.
Thy griefs are mine. But spite thy welcome sweet
I may not cross the steps of thy retreat.
See, from my head-gear bound against the wind,
The belt that I about my tunic bind,
The sandals on my feet, my staff in hand,
A man in haste to leave the routes of land.
My ship, and I to do my sire's behest,
Leave port and seek the waters of the West.
Below, even now, she scents the harbour bars,
Her master runs sweet water in his jars.
I came. But I must go: our wingèd sail
Gains the high seas ere yet the stars prevail.
To Paestum, guided by their heavenly host,
We bear dark wines of Thera from this coast.

Daphne.
Leave me not yet! So sweet the hour's mood!
Vast is the sea, cruel my solitude.

Hippias.
Hopeful I took this path at evenfall

To see thy door, thy shadow on the wall.
Ere long, retracing this my prospered road,
Thy father I will seek in thine abode,
To win thee hence, flatter his smiling age,
Drink from his cup, and thus his word engage
To make thee mine, thee, crowned with myrtle, borne
Across the sea where smiles the bridal morn.
O wine, O song, O flowers! Festal day!
Well do I see that Love will not have nay!
Through thee I know a maiden's hand is strong
To pierce man's heart—nor let it bleed for long.
Love is an ill, they say, but sweet to me
The love I bear, the pains I have of thee.
Woman thou art and bringest pain and weal,
Sweet as the rue, as powerful to heal.
For love is not for ay a troublous thing.
Under one roof our married joy shall bring
Peace and prosperity to the sacred hearth,
Children, and friends, and prudence against dearth.
There will we live like rooted trees and twin,
Kindly to all, and growing more than kin.
But at my father's word I go my ways;
Honour thy parent and see length of days.
Call upon Hesperus my path to keep—

DAPHNE.
Jesus I pray, who walked upon the deep.

HIPPIAS.
Daphne, thy words are heedless and to blame,

Call not on any god of alien name.
That gods are here in field and wood and skies
The breath that stirs them plainly testifies.
The breeze of Heaven breathes their word and sign,
I may not else than serve their ancient line.
Men of old time whose worth was more than ours
Rendered the homage due their jealous powers.
Pious as they from them receive the torch,
And pray, as they, erect within the porch.
Daphne, our gods are kind, and smiling, mate
The blushing maiden with the man elate.

Daphne.

On that dear day my hand in thine was laid
Thy golden ring enslaved a Christian maid.
A priest, who chased the naiads from a spring,
By salt and water gave me christening.
His I became, and His myself I count,
Sister to Him who died upon the mount.

Hippias.

What God may be, a man may not divine.
Let us abstain from slighting any sign.
For gods ambrosial-lipped we yet adore
Who came to us of old from Asian shore.
I, who am neither feather-brain nor clod,
Can well believe your Jesus may be god,
But since he died while yet the shadows kept,
Adonis he, whom Cytherea wept,
And Hermes he, because he showed a way

Out from the fields of Night into the Day,
Love and rejoice, O cherished head and fair!
The anchor strains, the sail lifts to the air.
Let my lips, parting, brush one golden tress—

    DAPHNE.
Another day, the kiss thou wouldst impress—

    HIPPIAS.
The blossom offers—
    DAPHNE.
      Wait until it ope.

    HIPPIAS.
Grant me remembrance.

    DAPHNE.
      Sweeter still is hope.

    HIPPIAS.
Thine eyes, these myrtles, all, enchain my heart.

    DAPHNE.
Go, fare thee well. Be sure the better part
Is ours.
    HIPPIAS.
   Alas, O maid! a livid dread
Upon thy smiling lips is to be read;
That pale smile bodes a future unbenign.

THE BRIDE OF CORINTH

DAPHNE.

The sea is in my thoughts, thy risk and mine,
The days of absence, the long nights, the dreams—
Thine image drifting, pale, in cold sea-streams.

HIPPIAS.

Thy tears have flowed, my lips have drunk thy tears.
Who fears the gods is freed from other fears.
Watch the four seasons bring their loss and gain,
Crowned with good fortune I will come again.

DAPHNE.

Friend, I will wait, and watch the changing year
As woman may, in her unchanging sphere.
I vow to thee that Death, and Death alone,
Shall, grudging, take what thou hast made thine own.

HIPPIAS.

Farewell, O Daphne !

DAPHNE.

   Hippias, part in peace !
        [*He goes.*
Hippias . . . mine eyes are dark, the clouds increase—
O misery ! O dread, unknown before !

Scene IV.

Daphne, Kallista borne on a litter. Her slave, Phrygia, accompanies her.

Kallista.
Phrygia, support me to the temple-door.
I sought thee, child. Oh, surely, God the guide
Who for His purpose brings thee to my side.

Daphne.
I gather herbs that may thy pains abate.

Kallista.
Child, to the heavenly mysteries dedicate,
Let be this vanity of earthly aid.
By other means my sickness must be stayed.
Hear me, my child. Thy mother, thou shouldst know,
Hath not her hope in this the life below.
Her bosom yearns for joys of Paradise,
And Death would come to her in joyful guise.
Not yet, alas, the hour of her release!
For who should guard the home, when I should cease,
From heathen speech and from the Demon's snare?
And who should, then, snatch him who is our care,
Thine aged sire, from out the yawning pit
His blindness opens 'neath his erring feet?

Thee, in the hour of thy soul's distress,
Weakened by milk of human tenderness,
What hand should pour thee spiritual mead ?
The many and submissive slaves I lead,
Lord, in Thy paths with sternness, then as now
Their feet must keep the furrow that I plough.
Whose voice, where gods of clay abound, O Lord,
Should keep Thy vineyards, spread Thy holy word ?
Who with just alms further Thy sacred cause
Among the pious poor who keep Thy laws ?
Thy will be done, O God, Thy will, not mine !
But ere Thou tak'st me hence, who am thy sign,
Forget not, Lord, these souls in grievous plight !
I am thy handmaid : grant me until night,
Mysterious Lord, to cultivate Thy vine,
That men may see the signal yield of wine.

Daphne.
Sweet mother, thou shalt live, and thy white hair
See length of days, and days secure from care.

Kallista.
I know thy love, my child ; the tender fear
That dares not hope and yet would keep me here.
God only can retard the hour for me,
Yet for my healing do I look to thee.
To keep me here some while if God consent,
I for His use must keep thee innocent,
Maiden, pure dove, lamb offered up to Heaven,
O chosen fruit, which God to me has given,

Plant which hast sprung beneath a love austere,
Not with the hope to put forth blossom here,
But to diffuse above a scent to please
The virgin God a vestal may appease;
Thy soul exalted by a boundless hope
No more may stoop within this narrow scope;
Thy lips now fevered with immortal lust
Thirst for the springs which never run to dust.
Life but a sojourn under veil of night
Thou keepest vigil, with joined hands, till light.
Child, though some earthly longing scarce expressed
At times has stirred the peace of thy young breast,
Thou couldst not sink to make a husband's bliss,
Nor meet the dust and ashes of his kiss.
Thou canst not wish, with pain and troubled breath,
To swell the harvest of man's sin and death.
Happy the widow, but happier the maid!
Happy is she who waited Him and prayed,
Turned with closed eyes from trust in carnal things.

Daphne.
To me a well-loved spouse my father brings.
Mother thou knowest he is dear to me,
Hippias of Thera, also loved of thee.
Wait a propitious day and better sped,
When thou art whole, to speak of him I wed.

Kallista.
My child, our earthly love is slight, and they

THE BRIDE OF CORINTH

Who love are coupled but by bonds of clay.
Christ's virgin, in the shadow of His house,
Shall find in ecstasy Immortal Spouse.
She then, His chosen, robed in bridal white,
Her heart transpierced, her forehead clad in light,
Hears to the harp and to the psaltery
The angels sing her bridal mystery,
Drains at the feast the chalice of God's grace
And, joyful, meets the ineffable embrace
That drowns her gaze, that, shining, waits the bride,
The Spouse whose bleeding Heart now opens wide.
Glory is hers if such a Master sue!
Hear what my soul is resolute to do.
The sacred portal's brazen folds afford
Me entrance! I address my sovereign Lord!
        [*She kneels upon the temple threshold.*
Here in Thy presence and Thy sanctuary
The just may seek the true electuary.
Under Thy porch and seven lamps of gold
Here on my knees I pray I may die old.
That I achieve my salutary task
In fast and exile here is all I ask.
Jephtha of old, if Thou didst hear his vow,
Mine Thy dear Son will surely hearken now!
I bring no blood-stained victim as the price,
Receive, O Christ, a heartfelt sacrifice!
I swear upon the word Thy Spirit sent,
I swear upon the fourfold Testament
Signed of the Angel, Eagle, Lion, Bull,
To offer in this bride exchange in full

For strength restored, health, and accepted vows—
Christ! I provide a maiden of mine house!
Let me but live! The child which blessed my bed,
Daphne, my daughter, to the altar led
That all may be accomplished as I swear,
Taking Thy ring and cutting her long hair,
Shall give herself to Thee, nor son of Eve
Sing epithalamy, nor she conceive.

Daphne.

Mother!

Kallista.

For she shall go, take Thee to spouse,
With girdle consecrate by jealous vows.

Daphne.

Mother!

Kallista.

And swear with faithful lips austere
No son of Adam ever shall draw near.

Daphne.

O Mother!

Kallista.

Yea, 'tis said, the oath shall stand!
King of the East, seated at God's right hand,
Christ! Oh, refuse not what I make Thine own!
Place on her stainless brow the veil and crown
That I may leave this world with length of days
Full of good works, my footsteps in Thy ways,

And see before me in God's sight, His train
Of angels harvesting my golden grain.
Behold her, this mine offering, of my breast!
For Thee I bore her, soon by Thee possessed!
When four-score days are passed and I yet live,
Strong for such service as Thy slaves should give,
It shall be sign, O King, that meet is she,
This maiden suckled in the fear of Thee!
A twelvemonth hence, at harvest-time on earth,
And she shall come to make Thine angels mirth.
Thy promised, pledged with ring of purest gold,
Fair, with veiled brow, to spousal joys untold.

Daphne.
Nay, mother, break this sacrilegious oath!
Release thy child whose tears should make thee loath
To bind her thus for ay, who prays thee now
To loose the toils of this so barren vow.
Oh, quickly, break this vow lest ruin swift
O'ertake us both for this thine impious gift.
Mind thee, oh, mind thee, of our former oath,
My father's word, the man I gave my troth!
My tender life deliver from the wraith
Of dread remorse which waits on broken faith.
Mother, the ring upon my finger set
To man derived from Adam binds me yet
To Hippias I yield my maidenhood.

Kallista.
Man's claim is naught—render all things to God.

DAPHNE.
Thy love—

KALLISTA.
In God I love thee.

DAPHNE.
Mother, hear!
Withdraw this network of remorse and fear
That I am taken in. Oh, set me free!
I ask for liberty to breathe, to be!
Listen! I saw but now my promised love
And promised here, with this blue sky above,
To follow faithful to the bridal room
Or pass with Charon in the bark of doom.
Have pity on me, nor forget the hour
Thy virgin heart first knew love's perfumed flower.

KALLISTA.
No visions fond my memory enslave.
But Love divine comes like a splendid wave
Wherein the heart in bliss and ravishment
Is rolled for ay in infinite content.
Love's longings burn thee, thee his thongs control;
Plunge in the flood of love thine ardent soul.
What I have done is done, nor lawfully
May any stand between my Christ and me.

DAPHNE.
It is accomplished. I am in thy snare.

THE BRIDE OF CORINTH

Kallista.

Even so.   And if an impious daughter dare
To violate the inviolable vow,
The debt I owe to God to disallow,
Spare, O great Judge, her consecrated head.
Visit on me Thy certain vengeance dread !
Unchain on me alone the shadowy fray
Of demons who unsleeping watch their prey.
May I lose grace nor at Thy table blest
Approach with cursèd mouth the sacred feast.
An alien to Christian work and deed,
Numbered no more, O Jesus, of Thy creed,
Mine eyelids shall be parched, and black despair
Burn like a flame the lips that know not prayer.
When like a ghost I haunt in my black night
The martyrs' tombs who shudder at my sight,
May the dark Seraphim and the Powers profane
Launch, under shock of broad funereal vane,
The sulphurous imprecation of their breath.
Without the sacred unction be my death.
No cross to kiss, no expiation be,
But Hell to shut for all eternity
Black on me, body and soul, plunged sixty-fold
In burning flame, in pitch and sulphur rolled.
They come !   I see the angels of the abyss !
My sin to thee now meets its Nemesis !
Daughter !   I feel their hairy grasp and stark.
I die—my soul is damned—and all is dark.

[*She falls senseles.*

PHRYGIA.

She is all cold and still and like the dead.
Wake thee, O mistress! Women, raise her head!
Her litter bring! Alas, how pale is she!
This wicked child has killed her, woe is me!

DAPHNE.

Enough! Bring ye the ring, the veil, the crown!
O Jesus, jealous prince—take then Thine own!
Mother, have hope, thy life is not yet stilled.
Oh, comfort thee, thy vow shall be fulfilled.
        [*Female slaves carry* KALLISTA *forth.*

SCENE V.

DAPHNE.

Dear Hippias, this vow thy clasp must sever,
Our union imperfect be for ever.
O thrice unfortunate, who found'st me fair,
Return no more, return but to despair.
Light not his way, O stars, to any port!
Breezes who swell his sails in gentle sport,
Night's mystic breath, if in you I may find
A soul and understanding dear and kind,
Visit his sacred bark who comes to claim
Me, who alas! may no more speak his name.
And if he sleep and dream of love and me
Let him not wake to bitter memory,

But sigh away my image from his eyes.
Let him forget! One day 'neath sunset skies
Some tranquil hearth may smile when he shall come,
Some maiden he shall find and lead her home.
Happier than I, if holding him less dear,
Ah, that 'twere possible. . . .

A distant chorus of youths, singing a bridal song.
   Hymen, Hymen, fair and fleet,
    Hesperus is high.
   Come, the darkened hours fly,
    Haste on shining feet.

    DAPHNE.
      . . . but I seem to hear
A choir invisible and far-off cries
Which hail a virgin to new-risen skies.

   The chorus draws near.
  Come, for night is short withal,
   Fit for lovers' vows.
  Hasten, bearing on thy brows
   Thy green coronal.

    DAPHNE.
With festal flowers, see, their locks are crowned,
For she has promised and is faithful found.

   Chorus nearer.
  Come, O ruler shod with gold,
   Hymenaios hail!
  See, the virgin yet is pale
   At thy greeting bold.

Daphne.

Friends come not near, oh, draw not nigh, dear
  friends.
Yet unadorned, though one on me depends,
On my sad brow no sweet amaracus
Entwines its heavy blossoms odorous.

The chorus goes its way, and—more distant . . .
  Beauty shines from out her form
    Meet for thine intent;
  Hymen, ever draw content
    From her bosom warm.

Daphne.

Where fades their song, where leads their festal
  rout?
My lover's friends will never seek me out!
Would I not, I, within the chamber brought,
Have spread a fragrance with ambrosia fraught?
Thine alien bride, O Hippias, will she prove
Of heart more faithful, better worth thy love?
O silent night, O lonely hour and cold!
On earth and on mankind I loose my hold.
  [*She detaches her gold ring from her finger.*
O fountain, where, men say, in days of yore
The nymphs knew depths of love beyond our lore,
O childhood's fount, O dear and sacred spring,
Receive a Christian maid's last offering.
O spring be faithful—in thy bosom cold
Hide for all time my loosened ring of gold.

With other hopes did I receive this ring.
            [*She throws her ring into the fountain.*
Rejoice, O God, who lovest suffering!

PART II.

The portico of the house of HERMAS. *The columns are covered with red stucco to within reach. The entablature is of white marble. Outside can be seen among climbing plants a Hermes in wood. Under a veil which screens the hot sunlight, women slaves are seated. Some are spinning wool, others weave stuff or broider hangings.* THEOGNIS *the bishop enters. He wears a low mitre and carries a crozier of white wood.*

SCENE I.

Female slaves, the bishop THEOGNIS.

THEOGNIS.
May peace be with you, daughters. At your sight
I know your hearts incline to do the right;
Busied about your tasks you clearly strive
Like honey-bees in a well-ordered hive.
Pleasing it is to see the shuttle speed
In hands that spin for those who are in need.
Praise to Kallista, mistress whose wise will
Orders such work and thus employs your skill.

Say, Phrygia, thou on whom her love is spent,
Is it, then, past, the malady which bent
The head and knees of one so strong in good,
Even as sleep dispels a troublous mood ?

[*Enter* KALLISTA—*the women slaves go away.*

SCENE II.

KALLISTA *and* THEOGNIS.

KALLISTA.
Bishop Theognis, peace be thine till death.
How doth this household, founded in the faith,
After the twelvemonth it must wait and yearn,
With all rejoicing welcome thy return !
O Pastor, let my hands embrace thy knees !
What kept thee, were it not the faithless seas ?

THEOGNIS.
A Tyrian vessel swift on agile oars
Took me unerringly to distant shores.
My dazzled eyes have seen that sight untold
Egyptian Alexandria, built of gold ;
Its citizens, its statued palaces ;
Its writings of the Gentiles and the wise
In cedar stored, a city of the dead ;
And, praised be God, have six times witnessèd
His Holy Word in contest overcome
The long-lived lie, tradition's foolish hum.

But to his flock the shepherd comes afresh.
The illness, then, that hath consumed thy flesh
Hath left thee, woman, and no longer grieves ?
God, at His will, afflicts us and relieves.
Restored to health thou think'st to pay thy vows
With tender gift, the daughter of thy house.
Thy welcome letter thus acquainted me.

KALLISTA.

What comes to pass I may not keep from thee.
Great things hath God accomplished for my good.
To thee I trust this child in whom my blood
Stirs, O Theognis, that thy saving hand
Ordain her lectrice in the novice band.

THEOGNIS.

Yea, I will lead her to the sacred house
As bride-elect of the Immortal Spouse.
But, thou art prudent, ere thou canst afford
An offering agreeable to the Lord
There needs a victim glad to pay the price,
A joyful heart, and prompt to sacrifice.
The virgin in the Canticles they bring
Perfumed with myrrh and sweet oils to the King :
In such wise should the bride of Him above
Exhale like precious nard her proffered love.
Say then, O woman, does thy Daphne grieve ?
Her family, her home, these can she leave ;
Her occupations, joys, and friends renounce,
All lingering hopes and loves permitted once ?

THE BRIDE OF CORINTH

Even as the traveller parts at break of day,
Girded her vestal robe, to take her way
Leaning upon the staff of Faith, where He
Awaits and calleth to her, "Come to Me!"

KALLISTA.

Know, then, my daughter, who abounds in grace,
No longer thinks or moves in this world's ways.
From mirth and tears withdrawn she long hath ceased
To share the pagan festival and feast,
Her father's joys. Sequestered all the year
She knows interior peace and silent prayer.
This vain and empty world she doth reject.

THEOGNIS.

Praise be to God! The mark of the elect!
The Master saith, "Who loves Me and would see
My Kingdom must leave all and follow Me."
To-morrow when the Lord His heavens shall fill
With stars, and night descend, and all be still,
When I have offered Divine Sacrifice
At martyrs' tombs who sing in Paradise,
My pastoral staff shall knock upon thy door;
At the third hour, then, welcome me once more,
Give me the child close-veiled and girdled well
That I may lead her whither God doth dwell,
And there her sacred hopes shall be attained
By imposition of hands and rites ordained.
O woman, thou shalt see her years increase,
Virgin and deaconess, and wax in peace,

Carrying folded in the linen stole
The bread of orphans and the widow's dole,
And offering each day the altar wine
The solemnizing priest shall make divine.
Glad tree, transplanted to the sacred sward,
To blossom and bear fruit before the Lord!
O woman, blessèd be thy womb, and blessed
The Holy Trinity thou hast confessed!

KALLISTA.
So may it be. [THEOGNIS *goes.*

SCENE III.

KALLISTA.

Chorus of vine-dressers singing in the road.
The god ferments, and, floating on the brink
Of the deep vat, our wooden cups are swirled.
O friends, I seem to be, the while I drink,
One with the gods, the masters of the world.

KALLISTA.
They chant their songs obscene.
Our song shall rise upon another scene
When to the heavenly vintage, child, we bear
Our purple grapes, where angel feet and fair
The fragrant must shall tread, and mystic wine
Flow thence, a liquor for the use divine.

Chorus.
If Myrrhina in mockery unbenign

Approach and laugh, and flee as flees the kid,
A naiad mingles with the blessed wine
Who loves me true, nor doth my kiss forbid.

Scene IV.

Hermas.

Crushed in the vat, the grapes spurt forth their
    blood!
Woman, thy thought is clouded by thy mood,
Though wits to thee the gods have not denied.
Surely the wife whose home is yet her pride,
Rejoiceth when the master's stores increase.
Be glad to-day and take thy proper ease.
A heavy vintage. Io! the black grapes
Brim o'er the press—the heady flow escapes;
Iacchus smiles. The household he befriends,
And the strong back of youthful manhood bends
Under the basket filled by smiling maids,
Maidens whose locks the leafy tendril braids.
They, too, sustain the heavy loads of fruit,
But in the winepress with light rosy foot
Tread not the grapes, where youths, and they alone,
Crush out the wine to song of measured tone.
For with firm foot the winepress must be trod
Ere the rich hidden juices will exude.
The elders, whose dry lips the wine anoints,
Feel a sly warmth unlock their stiffened joints;
They dance and shake abroad their hoary hair,

In shade of woods the maiden sleepeth, fair.
The young man goes in quest. Iacchus bids,
Inciting him to do unlawful deeds.
Let us enjoy the good the gods provide !
And Daphne, she my glory and my pride,
Daphne, my daughter, crown of mine old age,
Should smiling come and in our joys engage.

KALLISTA.

Hermas, our real joy in suffering lies,
It but seems sadness to your human eyes ;
Holy it is and hidden. " Watch and pray "
And " Woe to the scoffer," so the Scriptures say.
Not as the widow, thou, who, comforted,
Goes to the feast, singing, with unveiled head.
Daphne with flowers for the banquet crowned
Drinks not with Gentiles when the cup goes round.
Hermas ! with mirth and song time goes apace,
The hour is nigh . . . none saved except by grace !

HERMAS.

I am no augur, and thy words remain
Unread—a mortal man must guess in vain.
The very Sphinx, fertile in riddled lure,
Enwrapped her rhymes in darkness less obscure.
Thy wits are troubled by some god, maybe ;
Maybe a charm or poison works in thee.

[KALLISTA *goes forth.*

Scene V.

Hermas.
Woman is often ailing and distraught,
And evil humours work upon her thought,
And, if at times she hath the gift to see
Things that the gods veil in obscurity,
Yet fury and raving speech and wantonness
Work in her blood and spoil her graciousness.
Such ill is held inspired; but all things ill
Mean that some god possesses us at will.
A god lends woman charm us men to tame,
A god, again, acquaints her youth with shame;
Yet in her spring a virgin's fancies roam,
For some old nurse, at nightfall, in the home,
Lets drop the distaff; her lips pendulous
Moisten no more the thread, but garrulous,
Tell of a fair god dying in his youth.
The wound smiles red upon the pallor smooth
Of his so comely side, fragrant as myrrh.
The maiden lists; she sees, the words so stir.
Of Dionea hears the old belief,
How with dishevelled hair unbound, in grief,
She calls and weeps; how by her sweet mouth touched
Awakes to life the dear god rosy-couched.
Women each year, though husbands look askance,
Thus weep Adonis with loud utterance,
And to the sounding cymbal, sad and slow,

THE BRIDE OF CORINTH

Go fill the shady groves with sounds of woe.
Others seek Krestos in sepulchral night.
Yet are these gods not fair in name or sight
Whom death hath spoiled, and who demand our tears.
The gods I serve are joyous. Hence these cares.
Give me dark wine, and spiced food to eat.

A slave approaches.

Child, deck my brow with hyacinth, and set
All Syrian perfumes on the maple board.
Zeus, and Lyaeos, thou his son, our lord,
Of this, your wine, I first libation pour
To you, then fill the flower-wreathed cup once more.
Wine wakens godlike thought in aged men,
And makes them live their happy past again.
Memory is sweet to one whose life was full,
Dead men drink not, their days are dark and null.
Mussels are good when eaten in the shell,
Shell-fish, moreover, child, grow plump and swell
When the new moon above their ocean bed
Lifteth her thin white horn far overhead.
Artemis walks with those who rule our sphere;
Her pale untainted face makes dark things clear.
Endeavour, child, to learn from such as I
Our gathered knowledge of the woods, the sky,
The clouds, the mountains, and the great grey sea;
Thou, when these mighty things inhabit thee,
Do thou thy task with swiftness and with skill
Like a good servant, none shall use thee ill.
I see a stranger nearing my abode

Welcome and salutation be bestowed!
The gods his guide. Run, child, whoe'er he be
Tell him his coming hither honours me,
And that my prosperous house shall pour him wine.

Scene VI.

Hermas *and* Hippias.

Hippias.
Greeting threefold, old Hermas, father mine!

Hermas.
Hippias of Thera, Lakon's son, well met!
Greeting! To kindly gods I am in debt
Who to my house restore thy cherished head!
And that these eyes, whence light has all but fled,
A happy dream should see, thee disembarked!
With a white stone this happy day be marked!
O son of Lakon, wreath of ivy green,
Ancestral vessels, cups of silver sheen,
Meat, and all fruits, and dark wine shall be laid
For thee, that, thy just hunger being stayed,
Thou mayst acquaint me, dear and honoured guest,
How fares thy father, first of men and best.

Hippias.
He tends his vine and oft he speaks of thee,
But years have sapped his vigour.

HERMAS.

It must be.
What thou art now so was he once. There rise
Old days, our early youth, before mine eyes.
Tall was he, of thy stature at thine age;
Of equal brow. The elders held him sage
Ere yet the virgin beard showed on his lip.
Firmly he bore the wine-skin on his hip.
For men in those days were more vigorous far,
And better men, than their descendants are.
He is a happy man, thy father! Good is life!
For from a mighty spirit we derive.
The boy will throw the knuckle-bones and jest.
The youth, the ardent blood within his breast
Unquiet, by dusk willows seeks the maid.
White-haired, with load of many years o'erweighed,
Within the porch, under the starlit night,
In wise discourse the old man takes delight.
Whether thy days bring honey or black gall
Accept the thread of life Fate spins for all.
He whose disordered passions end his breath
Hath wished to live, and known not life but death.
Beware of vain desire and keen regret.

HIPPIAS.
Great longing fills my heart, for it is set
On her who is thy daughter, honoured friend,
On her I love and on the wished-for end.
My heart is hers, in her my sole delight.
Far have I roamed, seen the Ausonian might,

THE BRIDE OF CORINTH

Tibur, Neapolis, Paestum, and the coast
Of far Anconia, lands the Caesars boast,
Gardens, arbutus groves, and mulberries,
And orchards rosy with all fruitful trees,
The bounteous corn-lands and the clustered vine
Turning the sunlight on the hills to wine.
The grape grows kindly in a loosened earth
Where rainy skies bring growth of barren worth.
I lent attentive ear to native speech,
But long the days and empty, out of reach
Was she I loved. The subtle fever waked
Me through long nights, my dry lips went unslaked.
Daphne my vision, her white arms, her hair.
Fair image, fevered dream! Our vows, our care,
Love's sighs! O Eros! winged prince whose grace
Touches the virgin's breast and her soft face,
Man's torment, and the smile on heaven's vault!
Hermas, forget not, when I ate thy salt
By the ancestral hearth that summer's day,
Thy promise I should bear thy maid away.
Her young affection she hath not denied.
I claim thy promise, and I claim my bride.
There waits for Daphne, more to me than gold,
An ivoried chamber in my vessel's hold,
Glittering gear and Orient tissues fine,
Goblets, and perfumes shut in onyx, shine
Of brazen vessels great, all he bestows
Whom the gods bless, on his expected spouse.
My hope it is, when we two leave your shores
To bend green boughs about the bending oars,

Decked with bright flowers thick strewn as are the stars
To cleave the happy air with blossomed spars.

Hermas.

No, verily, my instinct hath not erred.
Rightly I gave her thee, my friend preferred!
For thou art just of deed and wise of word,
And with our ancient law thy ways accord.
Where counsel shall be sought, or deeds be done,
Thou yet shalt prove to be thy father's son.
Daphne, my child, is fair, and skilled, in sooth,
In all that may employ the timid youth
Of maids who keep the shadow of the house
And save their flower for their proper spouse.
The best to the most worthy should incline,
The straight young elm support the clinging vine,
And honey lend its sweetness to the strength
Of wine. But human hopes prove vain at length,
And fickle minds are caught unendingly
In the strong toils of our harsh Destiny.
Friend, it would grieve me were thy soul distressed
With heavy words, and fears but half-confessed.
Some breath of ill, some humours sprung of naught,
Weigh on my child and sombre all her thought.
She shuns mine eyes which in her beauty took
Refreshment, and drew pleasure from her look.
She speaks not, hides, and weeps. One well may know
She suffers not from any earthly woe.
She is possessed, some demon holds her heart.
The Galilean god hath played his part;

And this dead god, whose ghost my Daphne haunts,
Loveth not lovers, nor their bridal chants.
He loves not life and ever finds his good
In want and thirst and barren womanhood.
There is one leads my daughter, leads her blind,
Helpless, to him who hates our human kind.
The gods thy mother took; we mourn her still,
Good Pythias; another, by their will,
Old as the many-wintered crow, is left
To gather years and be of sense bereft.
But this late hour ill suits my train of years
I will go close mine eyes and lose my cares.
Hesperus, the lovers' star, now shows, benign,
Low in the western sky, his torch divine.
Sleep in security beneath my roof,
O son of Lakon! On thy couch, though proof
The narrow door against the midnight dew,
Spread this great lion skin of tawny hue.
Libykos of Cirta gave it me of yore
When in the year of Daphne's birth he bore
Coral, ivory, and copper to Hellenic strands
And took hence corn and wool to foreign lands.

Hippias.

Serenely I shall sleep on this fair couch
For Daphne's faith her plighted word may vouch.

Hermas.

May the gods watch thee, and thy sleep adorn
With happy dreams from out the gate of horn.
     [*He leaves by an inner door.*

Scene VII.

Hippias.

Stretched on the welcome couch with closed eyes
I feel the billows' gentle fall and rise.
Still hear the thresh of oars against the gale
And the wind moaning in the bellying sail.
The gleaming sea, blue capes and skies of blue
And fabled monsters, dance before my view.
A goddess shape my swimming eyes see now,
She floats mid heavenly airs before the prow,
Sports with the dolphins, ambient as air,
Touches the silver sands, a blossom rare,
Flees like a sunbeam; and the colours fade;
For, by the will of Love, I love a maid.
Doth this old man speak sooth? And wherefore should
This Galilean god in adverse mood
Now, when at length the golden hours atone,
Dispute with me the bride so hardly won?
I wrong not this young god of recent fame,
I have not spurned his altar or his name,
Have not affronted his ascetic priests,
Nor wantonly surprised their midnight feasts,
Their mysteries amid the tombs begot.
He cannot hate me; for I know him not.
Yet Daphne, silent, weeps and languishes.
Unholy is the grief whose sombre stress
Bows the white neck of one of Venus' doves.

But grief still more endears the friend one loves.
Perhaps the fault is mine her heart is sore;
Perhaps she fears I may return no more,
Forgetting that the virtuous gods assure
Safe conduct to the man whose heart is pure,
Who purified by every solemn rite
Hath made his vow and kept it in their sight.
To-morrow's dawn will bring her love again
And her fair brow relax its anxious strain,
And her eyes smile. O Zeus, thy sacred day
Lighten the form I love with earliest ray!
Artemis, hear me, have me in thy hold!
And thou, O goddess fairest, crowned with gold——
          [*He sleeps.*

Scene VIII.

The dream of Hippias.

Artemis *and* Aphrodite.

Artemis.

Oh, never more the darkling hours
Under the shifting moonlight sweet
Shall see amid the hawthorn flowers
The shining of my silver feet.

Aphrodite.

The sea, less supple than my thighs,
Than mine eyes' lucid depths less deep,
No more shall see my white shape rise
Bright upon memoried shores asleep.

THE BRIDE OF CORINTH

Artemis.
No more be mine the gift of grace,
Of strength, of beauty, as of old,
To youth the flower of the race,
Upright and chaste within the fold.

Aphrodite.
Lovers, all they who hailed me queen,
Now must they lose, nor re-acquire
The primal gift : the peace serene
In the inevitable desire.

Artemis.
The maiden in the untrodden ways
A tender growth beneath God's doom,
Shall learn, in innocent amaze,
That she came sullied from the womb.

Aphrodite.
Woman shall dread her beauty's snare ;
And find sweet love a bitter thing,
The sons of this new race, in fear,
Flee her, in deserts cowering.

Artemis.
O youth whose dreaming head and chaste,
Is pure as flower of the grass,
Come, that thy shining brows embraced,
Lighten the shades whereto we pass !

APHRODITE.

Oh, follow me—my gifts enjoyed
Have filled thy heart an hundredfold.
What dost thou here ? the gods avoid
A world that weeps in languor cold.

ARTEMIS.

Oh, follow me to crystal skies
And live immortal there, as we !
Away ! My chlamys, lover-wise,
Soft touches on thy yielding knee.

APHRODITE.

Let us away, lo ! even now
My veil and girdle kiss thy side.
Eternal beauty shall endow
Thy purer essence sanctified.

   [*They kiss him, make sign that he shall follow them, and vanish in the air.*

SCENE IX.

HIPPIAS *asleep*. DAPHNE.

DAPHNE (*she comes from an inner door*).
Since I at dawn, close-veiled, and habited,
Follow this aged man whose cross shall lead
My steps within the sacred shade, alone,

THE BRIDE OF CORINTH

And Christ's peace fall upon this heart of stone;
Since I must leave this world and, living, die,
Torn from its clasp, I yet would say good-bye.
When all yet lay beneath the spell of sleep,
I drew the wooden bolt, my chamber's keep,
With trembling hand, ere yet the night was sped,
And, fearful, stole from out my maiden bed.
Now hail thee, earth! and heaven, and wood, and sky,
And thee, old house, dear home, in days gone by
Given to mirth and song, and joy benign.
O door, O lowly porch, where leaves entwine
Old Hermes watching, carved of lemon wood,
Favour this visit—not to be renewed.
Abode so filled with mirth my natal year,
And thou, the roof-tree's stay, the column where
My father yearly marked my growth, and read
With joy the increase of my springing head!
White stones, on feast days fragrant, and in days
When I was small so close beneath my gaze,
Where my blue-armoured scarab, held in thrall
At a thread's end, would climb along the wall,
Or where small pliant twigs I would engage,
And hold my brown cicala in a cage!
And thou, O watchful lamp, farewell for ay!
               [*She opens the outer door.*
O you I loved, sleep on, sleep silently;
Dear hounds to whom I gave sweet cakes to eat,
Oh, bark not, springing up on hasty feet;
Shake not your collars, watch-dogs, nor resent
The footfall soft you know so innocent.

THE BRIDE OF CORINTH

I wish to run afield, to hear again
The leafage sound above the fountain-rain.
Yes, for the night is kind to innocence,
Out by the road, now fragrant to the sense,
With floating hair brushing the myrtles low,
To the nymphs' sacred fountain will I go,
To hear once more beside the waters cool
The slender reed-flutes, singing, pitiful.
I know a seat, a mound beneath the yews,
Whose turf mysterious night with love bedews . . .
Oh! I speak wildly!—nevermore for me
The fountain cool, the shade of friendly tree.

    HIPPIAS (*waking*).
Artemis, and thee, O crownèd Queen, I hear,
But what this sad sweet voice all thrilled with fear,
Your singing softly echoed in a sigh?
I wake, and on the moonlit threshold nigh,
Vague and white-veiled, I see a shadow move,
I see—O night! I see the one I love!
No shade intangible, no spirit form,
'Tis she! Love's very self, her presence warm!
    [*He rises and stretches forth his arms.*
Daphne, O Daphne! Sweet hour come at last!
My Daphne, come, O friend, a friend thou hast!
The kindly gods rejoin our destinies.
I thirst and hunger for thy love-lit eyes.
Under the choirèd stars God guides thy feet!
Daphne, I bring thee joyful news and sweet.
Thy vigil and my labours are at end.

We shall be one, thy father is my friend.
But what is this? Dost thou not hear, nor see?
What fear can chill thee, hold thee thus from me?
Speak. Do not flee me; fear not, but rejoice;
I am thy Hippias; know'st thou not my voice?

   DAPHNE (*speaking to herself*).
Angels! Oh, have me in your garments' fold!
Wherefore this cruel trial, grief untold,
To show me him whose vision is forbid?
I would regain the darkness where I hid.
But how, despite him, reach my maiden room?

     HIPPIAS.
Listen! O virgin, breathing sweet perfume!
I will speak softly, wait for thy replies,
Come to mine arms and speak, give me thine eyes!

     DAPHNE.
O guest, respect my passage, leave me free!

     HIPPIAS.
My face is browned with sunlight and the sea,
But friends long severed by an adverse star
May know each other still for that they are.
O trust thine eyes, the light of those twin stars
Bright as when early dawn the east unbars.
Dear child! Oh, trust what to thine ears is told,
Whereto I hang my vows as pendant gold.
Believe the spirit in thy gracious breast,

THE BRIDE OF CORINTH

Whose grace divine thy fairest thoughts attest;
I am thy Hippias; I offer my embrace.

DAPHNE.
Stranger, withdraw; I do not know thy face.

HIPPIAS.
Why speak'st thou thus, O girl? Oh, can it be
Some god, in blinding cloud enwrapping thee,
Hath wished, in wrath, to bring bewilderment?
Certes, some god must blind thee, ill-content
From lack of wine and honey-cakes and meal,
Hermes, or she to whom the Cypriotes kneel,
Or the dark Hecate. Their power, allowed,
May strike with madness him whose heart is proud.
Yet time restores our reason to its seat.
Listen, and I will speak in words more meet.

DAPHNE.
I may not hear thee, stranger, let us part.

HIPPIAS.
Daughter of Hermas! Light is the maiden heart;
Woman has moods, it is a woman's due.
My words shall breathe the sweetness of the rue.
I will recall our love to thee, and how
I first beheld thee; precious memory now!—
Beside the porch where golden sunflowers rise,
Needle in hand, with looks of sweet surprise.
Irresolute I stood. "Go, nurse," thou saidst,

"And give the stranger welcome to our midst."
Thy gentle words my inmost being thrilled,
I then knew love, O maid in beauty veiled!
But with my coming came the glowing swarm
Of playful loves to stir thy bosom warm.
Often a blush the lowered lids would own;
Often, O Daphne, the old bench of stone
Saw thine industrious hands forget the thread
At waning hours when all the west was red,
And the birds sought their nests under the beam.
For I, dear maid, would tell thee tales, their theme
My distant voyages, my dangers run,
Prodigies seen and men and cities known.
Then came desire and fret, and love's pursuit,
Thy pledge more sweet than honey is, or fruit;
Thy father's smile indulgent, thy lament,
My going—my return; the flowers' scent
When the hid naiad, the myrtles, and dark yew,
Heard thy sweet speech and took thy vows anew.

DAPHNE.
Oh, peace! Oh, peace!

HIPPIAS.
     I see thy quivering form,
'Tis thou, thyself, thy blood and body warm.
My love is in thy veins, thine every nerve.
Come! Oh, dismiss these fears that nothing serve
For love is life—love me.

DAPHNE.

                          I may not. Peace

HIPPIAS.

Why speak such words, my terror to increase?
Thy speech is touched with some inspired fear.
It holds thee cloaked. What mystery is here?
Reply, reply! Oh, tell me, what dread Fate,
What troubles dire thy heart so agitate?
Under the stars, before their Queen, the moon,
I pray and I beseech, O maid! This boon
With outstretched arms here at thy feet I sue,
Thou canst but grant the grace that is my due.
None but the wicked, in their madness set,
Reject the hand which supplicates its debt.
Let me embrace thy feet, thy hands, thy hair,
Tell me: thy wish is mine, thy joy I share.

DAPHNE.

Oh! Touch me not, or I shall be undone.

HIPPIAS.

No! The assent I hoped is not yet won.

DAPHNE.

Away! Oh, flee me!

HIPPIAS.

              Take but my embrace.

DAPHNE.

Oh, woe is me! And woe to thee! Disgrace—

HIPPIAS.
Oh, say what bodes this cry instinct with dread ?
How pale thy face, whose sorrow may be read ;
Thy startled eyes are wide with terror fell.
Oh, hateful silence ! Speak ! Oh, tell me, tell
The Iolchian magic, and the deadly brew,
What charnel compost, draught of livid hue,
What spells have touched the flower of thy face
And left this deadly pallor in its place.
What drug has frozen thus thy flesh and blood,
Charmed thee and left but thy similitude ?

DAPHNE.
Loose my hands.
HIPPIAS.
No. Thine ill is from above :
Earth doth not bruise the gentle flower of love.
Thee I adjure, O Daphne ! In these arms
Reply : what jealous god would steal thy charms ?

DAPHNE.
Enough. I love thee. Hence !

HIPPIAS.
I knew it so !
Necessity still leads, where'er we go.
Dost thou not feel her iron arm divine
Compel thine ardent breast to fall on mine ?

DAPHNE.
I fail !

HIPPIAS.
    Be docile, and submit to Fate,
Daphne, therein all beauty is innate.
Thy softness is thy beauty in love's eyes.
Yield thee, O child, for Love demands the price.

DAPHNE.
Leave me.
        HIPPIAS.
      I will not leave thee, but will rest
Till thy lips tell the trouble of thy breast.

DAPHNE.
O mitred priest, whose blameless hand must slay !
Mother ! Thy healing at what price I pay !

HIPPIAS.
Shrink not from telling me this mystery.

DAPHNE.
O sealed vow, O snare wherein I die !

HIPPIAS.
What is this vow ? I wait in anguish sore.

DAPHNE.
Hippias ! Live ! Farewell. I am no more.

HIPPIAS.
Oh, peace ! Call not on Hermes, god forsworn.

Daphne.
Jesus, O sacred ram, of brazen horn,
Who lead'st thy lambs where living waters flow.
Through what hard deserts must my footsteps go!
Eternal dolphin of the eternal sea
Behold my storm-tossed bark and pity me!

Hippias.
What speakest thou of Christ, what is thy thought?

Daphne.
Thy bride is His, though Him I have not sought.

Hippias.
'Tis Christ would snatch thee from my jealous hold?

Daphne.
His I become, He is the spouse foretold.

Hippias.
But what thy fate if such a Lover claim?

Daphne.
Live like a little child, and die the same.

Hippias.
O God of Galilee, unsought thy wrath!
Phantom unbidden risen on my path,
Whose threat'ning hand shows its ensanguined trace!
Hear me, dark Ruler of a sullied race:

Thy name I honoured, though unreconciled,
I marked not, Christ, because of this dear child,
What, of Thy story, age and wisdom said.
Heeded not reason nor the omens dread;
I thought thee good, a god withdrawn apart,
Of lofty mind, man's welfare at Thy heart.
I know Thee now, fierce spirit unappeased,
Envious spectre, who troublest thus the feast,
Power malign, striking at human kind
Who groaning walk Thy path, to tears resigned;
Unlawful overlord of magic might,
O Prince of death, whose cold strength serves to blight
Warm love, and chill the virgin at man's breast!
Thou art divine! Then hear my mind confessed,
And take Thy joy in what I have to say:
Here I await Thee, come, and seize Thy prey!
Take if Thou wilt, but in Thy hand bring Death,
Thou shalt not take her while I draw my breath.

Daphne.

Dear Hippias, peace! Most sinful is thine ire.
Blaspheme not! Dread its expiation dire.
Jesus of Nazareth thou hast belied,
That we might live, upon the cross He died.
He has not asked this sacrifice I make,
And she who gives me does so for my sake.
My mother sought my glory and my good
When she made vow to offer me to God.
Her honeyed hope proves wormwood of despair.

THE BRIDE OF CORINTH

HIPPIAS.

Daphne, the gods are good, nor hear the prayer
Of one who would forbid her daughter bring
The man she loves her virgin offering.
Begetters of the world! You do not heed
The mother who denies her daughter seed,
Would see her childless, loveless, and forlorn,
By alien hearths, and pointed at in scorn,
A useless burden on the teeming earth.
This earth where all things love, and bring to birth;
Stretching her sapless arms denied embrace,
Wandering, aimless, like a shade in space.
And shall that maiden beyond others dowered,
With Aphrodite's gifts divinely flowered,
One who already heard the amorous lure,
The words that fired to love her bosom pure,
Daughter of Hermas, glory of earth and crown,
Be left to wither sterile and alone?
They would not if they could, forbid our bliss!
Trust in the gods, O maid, and trust my kiss!

DAPHNE.

Alas! O trouble, madness, failing will!
Herbs of Iolchos, whose dark roots distil
The livid poison's dread paralysis,
Would work my ruin less than such a kiss.

HIPPIAS.

It comes from me, thy spouse predestinate.

Daphne.

Oh, fear to touch me, I am consecrate.
I fear myself, I fear God's part in me.
For the last time, farewell! I love but thee!

Hippias.

What love immortal equals love like mine?
I suffer and my sorrow is as thine.
No god can suffer, or can die for thee,
Unhappy child! Such kiss thy death must be.
O soul of mine, there is no such caress
As that of mortals clinging in distress.
No joy ethereal worth my kiss impressed,
Thy beauty, yielding, conquered, on my breast,
Thy tears!

Daphne.
    O spirit, spread thy dove-like wings.
I fail! Oh, lend the strength Thy presence brings!

Hippias.

How sweet is love.

Daphne.
   My love will not be stayed.

Hippias.

It is Love's wish: his law will be obeyed.

Daphne.

Dear Hippias, thou hast conquered. I avow

I love thee and am thine. Take me then, now.
Possess me. Let us flee, but hold me hid,
I follow thee and do what thou shalt bid.
Oh, that I rode through rushing air the plain,
Drank with closed eyes thy breath without restrain,
Would that I had a swift steed to my hand—
Oh, tarry not, but come. Leaving the land,
Flee to the gulf where thy bark rocks her spars.
I fear nor winds nor waves 'neath other stars.
Our bridal song, O friend, towards other shores
The chant of sailors and the sounding oars.
Ploughing the starlit waves thy vessel fleet
Carries me couched in shadow at thy feet.
Thou my salvation, thou my hope and faith,
My soul and being thine envelopeth.
Come! But alas for me! What have I said?
My speech is shameful—and my madness sped.

Hippias.
Maiden, thy love is virtuous and good,
I am thy promised; show thy friends like mood.
Yes, we will tempt the deep sea; and its wave,
Fair as love's self, and fruitful to the brave,
Shall gently bear our blameless destinies
To sheltering roof, where incense-smoke shall rise
Daphne, thy father's word shall stand in proof.

Daphne.
Master in whom I hope, beneath thy roof,
Father august, ageing in honoured ease,

We twain will seek thee and embrace thy knees . . .
No, we but dream, imprudent our belief
And hope deceived but aggravates man's grief.
My mother cannot loose her daughter's ties,
She will not ask for aught that Law denies.

Hippias.

Thy mother is no heartless savage wild,
A woman's milk has fed her when a child,
Only the cruel gods impassive see
Our human misery: but, mortal, we
Know pity, for our suffering makes us heed.
What mother hears, except her heart must bleed,
That child on whom her pains did life confer
A second time demanding Life of her?
A mother yields to tears; yet mortal she.
We will go to her, humbly bow the knee,
Our prayers, our raisèd hands, our tears shall speak,
And pity at the last shall smooth her cheek.

Scene X.

Hippias, Daphne, Kallista.

Kallista *enters, a lamp in her hand.* Daphne
hides her head on Hippias' *breast.*

Kallista.

What are these cries? Who, in this chaste abode,
Moveth when unclean spirits are abroad?

What suspirations shame, what kisses taint
This house and through the solid walls acquaint
The air with vapours of disease and death?
Man, wouldst thou violate, with drunken breath,
One of my household whom I guide aright
Through the day's heat and shadows of the night
To the celestial city's living walls?
Wouldst thou, then, shameless, force my female thralls?
But no—I plainly heard your spoken word,
Your voices mix in hideous accord.
God! That beneath these eaves the Demon lust
Should set his red imprint, and straightway must
A Christian woman, stung to appetite
At one bound, seek a stranger's bed at night!
On thy knees, woman, whoever thou mayest be,
Thou whom an unclean spirit, inhabiting thee,
Hunts thus by night, maddened, on heat, a-gog;
Bitch, whose throat howls for every wandering dog,
The leathern thongs, the salutary whip
Shall dominate thy flesh, and hush thy lip!

Hippias.
The majesty of years adorns thy brow,
O woman, but too swift to wrath art thou.
Beneath this roof my brows were ivy-crowned,
I leave unsoiled the welcome bed I found.
No slave has mounted sly and stealthy-stepped
Like a foul nightmare where the stranger slept.
Within my heart an honest purpose bred.

Calm thyself, woman ; see thy child's chaste head
Her whom I love, who loves me—

KALLISTA.

O amaze !
A poisonous vapour must becloud my gaze.
'Tis she, I see her ! Thou, a Christian maid !
A Gentile, and his hand on thine is laid !
Abomination ! Christ, where art Thou, then ?
Where sleeps Thy sword, Thy virtue, far from men ?
O Christ, but see him ! See, O King, and smite !
Thy portion feels his touch, Thy fruit his bite.

DAPHNE.
I will not live without him. I die first.

KALLISTA.
Man sacrilegious, vile, of God accurst,
I drive thee forth—go from this pious house.
Flee, nor breathe poison on her youthful brows.
Flee, in all shame, thy head within thy hands,
Seek in the shades where any path expands
Thy shelter fit, in any sink of night.
Bestir thee, or the rods shall speed thy flight.

HIPPIAS.
A furious demon agitates thy frame
And froths thy lips. I go, as erst I came,
O woman, bearing high an unbowed head.
But with thy guest thine honour thou hast sped.
Thy roof whence now the ill-omened bird shall cry

THE BRIDE OF CORINTH

Sees the insulted guest depart, and with him fly
Innocence, Faith, and Peace, triad august.
And holy Piety, and Laws held just.
Mine is her soul which thou canst not constrain.
Zeus grant me triumph when I come again.

DAPHNE.

Hippias!

HIPPIAS.

O Daphne!

SCENE XI.

DAPHNE, KALLISTA.

KALLISTA.

                I will wash each stone,
His scandalous feet have touched, and make atone.
I know, my child, that God upheld thy faith
Already trembling at his unclean breath.
Against the tempter fasting is thy shield,
And Jesus' name the spear that thou must wield.
To rule the flesh so prompt to disobey
Let us prostrate ourselves and groan and pray.
Humbled in dust and ashes let us bend
Until the grace and blood of Christ descend.
My daughter, one more day, and then the Ark
Shall open and the bride of God embark,
Thy soul be sheltered, and thy robe made sure
From stain of sin in this dark age impure.

I see, I hear. The Son of Man is come;
And Adam's seed is rising from the tomb
And knows Him. Lo, the hour! The Angel's flail
Beats out the grain and chaff to meet the scale.
The heavenly trumpets rend the firmament.
Child, let us flee this world indifferent.
See, the Judge cometh in a reddening light!

DAPHNE.

O mother, leave me. I am slain outright,
Mine eyes already see the dark increase.
I sink upon the hearth to die in peace.

KALLISTA.

My prayer and torment shall avert the curse.

SCENE XII.

DAPHNE, *later*, *the* NURSE.

DAPHNE.

Kharito! Kharito! Come, mine ancient nurse,
List! Hippias of Thera thou dost know
Thy Daphne dies unless thou hear'st her woe.
Thou canst not wish, good nurse, to see me dead.
Chased from the house my Hippias is fled.
His love for me will make him slow of flight,
Regret will weight his sandalled footsteps light.
Excellent Kharito, nurse who cradled me,
Quicken thy heavy limbs, and hasten thee.
Follow his footprints on the sandy ground,

Run to the spring, and seek him, and when found,
Tell him to wait me when the stars once more
Throw the pine shadows on the forest floor
By the great tomb which iron gates enfold.
Thou tarriest : hasten, run : for time is gold.

Nurse.

My child ! I go. Though truly it were best
If I abstained from such inglorious quest.
Thou hast my love, and sometimes for our friends,
We must pursue and seek unlawful ends.

Daphne.

Run and return. By adverse fates misled,
My funeral couch shall be my marriage-bed.

PART III.

Night. A wide and shady road. At the side of this road a tomb half hidden among pines. One sees the interior of the monument, the funeral chamber. Niches hollowed in the walls holds urns with ashes. Round the interior runs a marble bench; in the middle is an altar.

Scene I.

A Wise Woman.

No farther ! Standing in a moonlit space
A tomb among dark pines, the appointed place.

58 THE BRIDE OF CORINTH

The iron gate is mute, heavy and dark;
No voice as yet, no step, no light to mark.
The maid is not far off, and come she will,
For I am sought and summoned for my skill.
Many the tears my withered hands have felt,
Many the kiss my furrowed brow would melt.
For I am dear to lovers, see them prone
Pressing the knees of this so aged crone.
In town and village every servant tells
The children of my knowledge and my spells.
Aye, I know more than all, and slowly starve.
Within my bones I feel the hunger carve.
Rest to the needy is a fruitless boon,
I must bestir me 'neath the friendly moon,
Tear from the tombs the roots whose virtue dread
Is nourished on the bodies of the dead.

Scene II.

The Wise Woman, *the bishop* Theognis, *followed by deacons and other faithful singing in Chorus.*

The Chorus of the Faithful.
Glory and praise in Thee, O Lord,
   To those of loyal blood,
Who by the lance, and blade, and cord,
   Witness Thy Name and Rood.

THE BRIDE OF CORINTH

An age perverse has set them free,
   We, groaning, pray and wait.
Grant us to wear, who yearn for Thee,
   Thy purple robe of state.

THEOGNIS (*to* THE WISE WOMAN).
Thou, whom I meet upon this road we tread,
Com'st thou to pray beside the martyr'd dead
With us, O woman, where lamps of life shine clear?

THE WISE WOMAN.
Man, I reply without deceit or fear.
I am a woman most miserable and weak.
Beneath these pines and maples tall I seek
Dead wood, to warm my poor old bones, and dry.

THEOGNIS.
Woman an-hungered and a-thirst, draw nigh!
"Blest are the suffering," Christ hath said. "The rich
For ay shall burn in sulphur and in pitch."
The hand that gives thee alms, this gold hath crost
In name of Father, Son, and Holy Ghost.

The Chorus of the Faithful.
Grant, Lord, the glory we desire
For which our life-blood flows—
To wear upon our white attire
The martyr's blood-red rose.
    [*The Bishop and the chorus move away.*

Scene III.

The Wise Woman.
Hate makes us twain.   Presents are nothing worth
I hate both easy men and grudging earth.
I hate whatever nourisheth a life within,
Both flesh and grass.   I cleave to Death and Sin.
My nails have dug the rooted plant away.
Hurry thy steps, my pretty child a-stray,
A rich old man is urgent for a charm
To bring him back his youth and nerve his arm.
He calls, and I, beneath my robe I hang
Whisker of wolf and serpent's poisonous fang . . .
Here is the child!   I shall have gold again.

Scene IV.

The Wise Woman, Daphne, The Nurse.

Daphne.
Nurse, take this key.

Nurse.
     There is still time—refrain.
My child, my blossom, hearken what I say,
We two are following an evil way.

DAPHNE (*to the woman*).
Woman, I seek the aid you swore to lend.

WISE WOMAN.
The aged wife is prompt to serve a friend.

DAPHNE.
Take, give—and leave me.

THE WISE WOMAN
(*gives the phial and receives a piece of gold*).
                    Here is weight and shine!
O tender maid, thy locks are fair and fine!
If so be that some youth is all thy care
Bring me, my dear, from him a single hair
And you shall see him, spellbound by my charms,
Woo thee with flowers, tearful—in thine arms!

NURSE.
Daphne, what saith this toothless wife to thee?
Most harmful to the young such hags may be.

DAPHNE.
Open the door, my nurse—how slow thy hands!
Haste with the light, the lamp expectant stands.
Be silent and obey.

           NURSE.
          It is not right

Nor nice, my child, to enter tombs at night.
His counsel just, the slave is rightly bold.

Daphne.

Set down the viands and the cups of gold
Upon our altar where of yore we made
Libation to the gods when passed a shade.

Nurse.

Childlike I act although I am a crone.

Daphne.

The bread and salt—'tis well. Leave me. Alone,
With mine own hands I mix the wine I need.

Nurse.

It is my duty, Daphne, and I heed,
But leave these tombs where the dogs howl and
  roam,
Seek the warm shelter of thy couch and home.

Scene V.

Daphne.

No, neither god nor friend shall be betrayed
By me, weak as I am, and sore afraid.
Even now I seemed to see, amid the gloom

In the dark dovecote, float on dusky plume
The shades of those who loved and went their ways
Under a happy sky in happier days.
They lived their lives, their ashes are at peace.
The terrors of this vigil now increase!
The air is thick with shades, their pressure nigh.
Oh, give me life, and breath, and sight of sky!
Vain wish! The time is now at hand—and he.
I must prepare the cup for him—and me.
I from this vase will drink where, graven, show
A virgin sleeping and winged babes who go
And come lightly o'erhead, and fly in aery troop.
    [*She opens the witch's phial.*
I pour what I must pour into this cup. .

Scene VI.

  Hippias (*on the road*).
Hail, all ye stars! In the dead tree's dark cleft
The hoarse crow spoke from the ill-omened left.
Just gods, avert this presage of ill-fate.
Shadowed by pines I see the dead men's gate.

  Daphne (*without seeing him*).
Dear Hippias! the midnight skies are dark.
The time is precious, but thou dost not mark,
Thou lingerest yet. Oh, come, I am prepared;
For thee my breast breathes perfume.

HIPPIAS (*at the gate of the tomb*).
                              Most endeared,
My Daphne, O my fate, Daphne my sweet,
Fugitive saint on fair and furtive feet!
The gods yet load with years the aged nurse
Who brought thy message to the flower-set source.
Thou art no child whom childish things control,
Thy heart courageous clothes a faithful soul.
Follow me, Daphne; rest thee, and confide:
I will be thine, thy refuge and thy pride.

DAPHNE.
Come, let us sit upon this marble seat.
Whatever chance the future may secrete,
Friend (for we know not what our fate may give),
We will no more be parted while I live.
In human lives bright hope may briefly shine.
Oh, lean thy shoulder, take my hands in thine!
One roof, one bed shall give us ample room,
My soul from out my lips thou shalt resume,
Shalt close mine eyes, receive my latest breath!

HIPPIAS.
Daphne, the gods conceal the hour of death.
Think of the present, gird thee, nor delay.
Hasten, they seek thee, they are near . . . **away.**

Scene VII.

Daphne, Hippias, *in the tomb.*

Theognis *and the Chorus of the Faithful repassing on the road.*

Chorus.
An age perverse has set them free,
  We groaning, pray and wait.
Grant us to wear, who wait for Thee,
  Thy purple robe of State.

Theognis (*to one of the deacons*).
Lo, now, when sleep bows every head, there shines
Light from their tombs who toiled in the vines.
The anxious vigil of the ruddy spark
Betokens theft, or rape, or workings dark.
Go, Dionysos, with light step and view
What deed is doing 'neath the pine and yew.
Go, for the guardian must supervise
Bad men whose crimes the dark hides from our eyes.

[*He passes on. The deacon* Dionysos *steals to the vine-grower's tomb, and sees, without being seen,* Hippias *and* Daphne. *He runs to rejoin the bishop, who has gone his way with the choir. One still hears the Chorus of the Faithful.*

THE BRIDE OF CORINTH

Chorus.

Grant, Lord, the glory we desire,
For which our life-blood flows,
To wear upon our white attire
The martyr's blood-red rose.

DAPHNE.

It is a Christian chant, the song whose flood
Mounts towards the saints baptized in their own blood.
Whither, O martyrs, floats your bright array?

HIPPIAS.

My mantle cloaks thy tender breast—away!

DAPHNE.

Hippias, believe this shelter sure—nor fear.
I wish, as it beseems, to make thee cheer.
Wine will we drink where sleep the blessed dead.
Seat thee, my Hippias, the feast is spread.
We celebrate our spousals, friend, here are
The chalice and the thin-necked water-jar,
The cups, the perfumes, salt, and wreaths of green,
Lilies, and frail anemones between.
As it is fit, before this honoured dust,
We feast our marriage in this banquet just,
Pale violets and hyacinths soft-spread
A perfume on thy triply-banded head;
From odorous vase the scented contents shake,
Wreathe these fair flowers on thy brow and take
This cup where mix dark wine and water bright.

THE BRIDE OF CORINTH

HIPPIAS.
In the lone tomb under the veil of night
With festal roses I adorn my head.
Daphne, I bow to all that thou hast said,
And my heart holds, with thine, that it is just
Piously to feast this union so august.
This wine to Hera, kind to wedded bliss,
This to thee, Cyprian, and to thee, Huntress, this,
And all you Loves who spread light wings at night,
Aid me to keep this spouse, fair-limbed and bright,
If ye would favour modesty and love.

DAPHNE.
I raise my cup in turn to Heaven above.
Thou, who, midst olives, from the cup didst shrink,
See me! I cannot, so my heart doth sink,
Alas! I cannot taste this bitter sup—
My lips dare not approach the golden cup.

HIPPIAS.
Drink, reach the cup that half thy draught be mine,
That I may taste thy sweet breath in the wine.

DAPHNE.
Hippias, I drink this wine—I must, I will.
See, in my hands I take this cup I fill.

HIPPIAS.
Drink to our union, friend.

Daphne.

                O destiny!
'Tis done! I drain the bridal cup to thee.
Henceforth, O friend, its service be forgot.
'Tis consecrate to Him thou knowest not.
I am not woo'd in delicate repose
'Mid sun and smiles and petals of the rose;
My love in nerves and blood and passion lost
Gives without stint, with death in the accost.
Thy shining eyes now bathe me in delight,
Thy locks resplendent and thy temples bright.
Hippias, the soft down my eyes close seek
Lies like a mist of morning on thy cheek.

Hippias.

About the flower of thy mouth I hear
Bees make sweet murmur, Daphne, to mine ear;
And sacred love fanning, with gentle gale,
Thy budding bosom flowers 'neath its veil.

Daphne.

Hippias, thy stature and thy noble brow
Make live the dream of heroes long ago.

Hippias.

Daphne, thy rounded arms, swift to enlace,
Bare themselves proudly from the robe's embrace.

Daphne.

Hippias, what courage decks thy bosom warm!

THE BRIDE OF CORINTH

HIPPIAS.
Daphne—of candid soul and goddess form!

DAPHNE.
I cling to thee!

HIPPIAS.
I hold thee to my heart!

DAPHNE.
Sweet!

HIPPIAS.
Flame of love!

DAPHNE.
     I feel my life depart ...
Oh, fold me close lest jealous Death divide
And unresisted snatch away thy bride.
Of nights old boatman Charon quits his bark
And rides the roads on a great courser dark.
When I shall wander where all bright things fade
Thy hands shall heap no offerings to my shade.
Where walk the Christian band their way is mine.
My spirit there may never welcome thine.

HIPPIAS.
Leave, then, this god who loveth not our feasts.
Love is the lord even of the savage beasts.

DAPHNE.
Christ Jesus will one day restore his own.

This is the doctrine to our sages known.
Thou, who art man, mayst ask and seek to know;
I, woman, must believe, and, silent, bow.
Christ, King of death—Blessed all names above!
This life is short, but infinite is love.

HIPPIAS.

O dear one, smile, nor speak these names of fear
To soil thy lips and shame thy sunny hair.
Tempt not thy fate thus, life is yet divine,
Love then, and live—the empty rest resign.

DAPHNE.

Live long, my Hippias, drink of the sun—
But dwell at times in memory, on the one
Who showed thee first—for love hath clearest eyes—
How fair is life beneath the clear blue skies.
O spouse of mine, treasure my solemn words!
When the dark couch where haunt the ill-omened
    birds
Receives—alas! this body once so dear,
When I am but a phantom thin and drear,
Cherish the memory of the Christian maid
Who once was fair, whose hand in thine was laid,
Who loved thee with no fickle heart nor light.
Sometimes, at home, one gives the fancies flight.
(Another, another, then, will fill the dearth,
And take thy dead love's place beside the hearth!)
A little space thy laughing darling leave
For the green garden's mossy seat, at eve,

And thou shalt see my shade above thee bow,
And feel, no kiss adulterous on thy brow,
But the wind's breath bringing my soft caress.
Thus may the dead the living yet address.
Borne on the breeze, heard in the rustling leaf,
Always shall I return though thou be deaf.

Hippias.

Virgin, the gift of words is on thy lips;
Inspired by the Muse thy soft speech slips
Between thy white teeth where the graces play.
But wherefore dwell on things unfit to say?
Why is the bridal robe with tear-drops pearled?
Youth, pleasure, and the brightly coloured world,
Love, all things, smile on us—and thou must weep!
Follow the light-foot hours so airy sweep!
Welcome our sacred joy in spirit light,
The world that gave thee birth, dear child, is bright!
Now thou art mine all things are sweet and dear,
Life will run gently for us, year by year,
Tasting each joy our destiny may bring,
Nor heeding future Fate's dark offering.

Daphne.

How sweet to seek the spring at heat of day!

Hippias.

Companion mine, we must pursue our way.
See, the stars slide from Heaven. Thy mantle gird,
Gain my sure bark, my sailors wait the word,

THE BRIDE OF CORINTH

And ancient Glaucos on the oar-swept seas
Shall see thee fly before the morning breeze.
Come, for the night fades : hasten us, and flee.
　　　　　　　　[DAPHNE, *pale, rises and totters.*
Daphne, thy fair form droops across my knee.
Ye gods ! What Lamia hath, with hands unseen,
Laid these pale violets on thy brow serene ?
A scent of death exhales within this lair,
Let us go forth and breathe the soft pure air.

SCENE VIII.

DAPHNE, HIPPIAS, THEOGNIS, KALLISTA, HERMAS,
and slaves bearing torches.

THEOGNIS (*to* HIPPIAS *and* DAPHNE, *who issue
from the tomb*).
Stay, children, learn by whom you are addrest :
I, in Christ's name, am shepherd of souls and priest
Of King Melchisedech's eternal line.
Without concern or fear your hearts incline.
I come not, child, to consecrate, in sooth
Christ will forgo this flower of thy youth ;
In a man's hold it shall its scent emit,
God, who is pure, hath no more joy in it.
The power to bind and loose is in this hand.
Hear me, O daughter, and all men understand,
Thy mother's vow I loose which else did bind,
Lawfully thou mayst unite thee with thy kind.

THE BRIDE OF CORINTH

Since for the Mystic Spouse thou art unworth,
Fear not, but follow, then, this son of earth.
For our dear Master took his place and blest
Miraculous wine at Cana's marriage-feast.
Thou, come of Gentiles, whom, the truth refused,
Falsehood makes wander like a man bemused,
Listen, that God may deign to bless thy bed :
Leave thine old ways, believe ; the Apostle said,
" The man who weds shall sanctify his bride
And the New Church this sacrament provide."
Ye would be wed ? It may be done, and can.
Man, take this woman. Woman, take this man.
In name of the Eternal and the Son
And of the Paraclete, in glory one,
I join you. Be one flesh in this your life,
Follow him, woman ; man, cherish this thy wife.
Render one day this child thou tak'st unspoiled
Back to her God, yet joyful and unsoiled.
Now ye are one exchange your rings in troth.
By laying on of hands I bless you both.

HIPPIAS.
O holy man ! Some god must walk with thee !
Nay more, thou seem'st a God. O prodigy !

HERMAS.
Certes, 'twas time these children were made one.
What thou hast done, O priest, was wisely done.
The great ox will I slay, my stable's pride,
And the red wine shall flow on every side.

All from the vines, all shepherds from the hill,
Shall throng your nuptials, children, in good will.

DAPHNE.
Prepare the feast, prepare the funeral feast.
God's snare has shut, my breath has nearly ceased.
Cruel, alas! The hand would liberate
To life and love now, when it is too late.

HIPPIAS.
Daphne, what evil threatens, yet untold?
I hold thy hand and yet thy hand is cold.

DAPHNE.
Farewell! For me the myrrh and winding-sheet.
Faithful to thee, O friend, could I yet cheat
God and my mother, and follow thee alone?
Think'st thou that love and life could all atone?
I came to thee because I might not live.
Hippias, my death is all I have to give.
Thou know'st the poison that the witches brew
From flowers Thessalian wet with midnight dew?
Its livid fumes I drained, my cup is dry.
Cold is my body, my arms droop—I die.

HIPPIAS.
Despair and woe! Flowers and coronals, fall!

DAPHNE.
What I have done is done, nor asks recall.
Know by my act how great the power of love.

THE BRIDE OF CORINTH

Grave in your minds what I so sadly prove,
And tell my tale, that never child be sped
By mother's hands to such dark bridal bed.
God knows I would have lived had He seen fit,
Earth smiled so bright. I would have joyed in it,
Known hearth and husband's care, and, fond and
  proud,
Nourished a child, and heaven had seen no cloud.
Love breathing soft, life waking to its play . . .
Innocent dawn is come. Friends, it is day.
Bear me, oh, bear me to the rosy hills
Where o'er the tamarisk the fountain spills . . .
The night returns, night wraps me, darkness shed.
Dear husband, take me, bear me to the bed
Where I may rest me in my robe of grace.
Hippias, thy hand must cover up my face.
Father, farewell. Thou whom I loved live on!

HERMAS.

Dead, O my daughter! For ever is she gone!
Woman, thou hast slain her! Say, what barbarous
  God
Has foamed thy mouth, ridden thee thus rough-
  shod;
Driven thee senseless, pitiless, to destroy
Thy daughter and myself and all our joy?
Cruel are men when the gods stir to wrath,
Widowed and childless I will flee this hearth.
Thy face accursed, my vine, my land that was!
Alas, my child, my flower! Alas, alas!

Kallista.

The mother's heart is piercèd with a sword.
God, grant me light, if I mistook Thy word.
Punish me, Lord, if I have sinned.   But no,
This that I did worked for Thy fame below,
Thy glory upon earth, the good of souls,
Thy love, whose flame my every act controls.
For a rich jewel I offer Thee each tear
I cry to Thee from out this sorrow drear
And my lips praise Thy wisdom infinite.
Thou tak'st my child—I bless Thee though Thou
  smite.

Theognis.

Thy vow was rash, thy zeal had made thee blind.
But thou hast faith, and shalt salvation find.
To the East turn we the dead woman's face.

Hippias.

Hold! she is mine.   I bear her from this place.
With her I fly before this ruin hurled;
Beauty and love have perished from the world.
Since all the earth is subject to strong Death,
I will seek light and life where none draws breath;
Fell the great pines and lay the woodland oak
That on one pyre our souls go up in smoke.
That we whom, while we meet the bright flame's
  face,
The steadfast earth-flax nets in one embrace,
May flee on fiery wings these drear abodes,
And seek the bosom of the distant gods.

HIPPIAS *of Thera*,

Son of LAKON.

Passer, be glad. Sacred this earth laid even
On one who served the gods his twenty years.
Two Loves are on this rough-hewn column graven:
One takes from men the light the one has given,
But both are fair and both smile on our tears.

Daphne,

Daughter of Hermas.

The Christian Daphne, by the times undone
Tastes in eternity, for her begun,
The joys of Jesus in the heavenly dawn.
Honey from bitter wormwood hath she drawn.
Her mortal part, to be reborn all pure,
Was laid by Christian kinsmen in this place.
If one profane disturb her sepulture,
   May he perish, last of his race.

NOTE

In the days of the first Cæsars a kind of delirium troubled all minds. Through the confused union of a tripartite world at once Roman, Hellenic, and Barbarian, the great roads opened by the legionaries gave passage to every sort of folly. There was free exchange of superstitions. Rome had long since picked up the morbid cults of the East. Prodigies from India, Thessalian enchantments, marvels of Africa, that fecund mother of monsters, and the Italiote practices of neo-pythagorism, were merged and confounded. From this was thrown off a curious haze which, spreading over the world, hid or mis-shaped all nature. The better minds were still ruled by a measure of education and knowledge. But a varied acquaintance and a subtle intelligence served them but to imagine wonders and multiply superstitions. Long voyages were willingly undertaken by the curious-minded. The roads were safe. A Roman citizen found sheltering institutions and well-disposed authorities in every town. Hosts to whom he had recommendation provided shelter and hearth according to ancient custom, whose exercise he facilitated by providing food for himself. On his way he visited ancient temples and sacred places, and let himself be initiated in the mysteries. Nothing less secret than such mysteries, nothing more fashionable than such initiation. And on very side rose wonders, oracles, and magic doings for willing ears and staring eyes. Sophists and rhetoricians, heard with avidity, contributed to the frenzy of men's minds. Their every discourse, as was said of those of Dion, spread abroad a perfume as from a temple. Phlegon the Trallian was a child of his age. Born in Lydia, that home of mixed races and diverse customs, an educated slave and freed man of the Emperor, the Empire, in its entirety, was his fatherland. He wrote, as it happened, a description of Sicily. He was made historiographer to the Emperor Hadrian, and certainly was annalist to a Cæsar of inquiring mind.[1] He compiled for a society mad on marvels and for a prince who was an astrologer, a *book of marvellous things*. These things were believed all the more willingly since they were utterly absurd. We have some remains of it, and notably a letter from a procurator to some official of the imperial *aula*. It is not hard to see that this letter is apocryphal. The first centuries of the Christian era abounded in pretended accounts. Forgers made Enoch speak, or Hermes. There was no criticism, and no suspicion. People wished to believe, and they believed.

Here is the letter which, so far as I know, has not

[1] Hadrianus, curiositatum omnium explorator (Tertullian).

THE BRIDE OF CORINTH

before been translated into French. The beginning is lacking. One may, with Xylander, restore its substance in some manner.

Philinnion, daughter of Demostratos and of Kharito, though dead, secretly joins a guest of the family, Makhates. The nurse surprises them.

... She opens the door, enters the guest-room, and sees, by the light of her lamp, the young girl seated by Makhates. Unable to contain herself at this prodigious apparition, she runs to the mother, calls her with loud cries and presses Kharito and Demostratos to rise and follow her and see their daughter. She has seen her, alive, and, at the will of some god, seated with the guest in the entertainment room. Kharito, when she heard this incredible account, was at first overcome by the gravity of the news and by the nurse's agitation, and was on the point of swooning. Then, the memory of her daughter supervening, she wept. Anyhow, she said that the nurse must be out of her mind, and bade her go away. But the nurse reproached her with losing, through such heedlessness, the chance of seeing her child. "For," said the old servant, "I am not mad nor have I lost my wits." At length Kharito, in spite of herself, half influenced by the nurse's insistence, half by curiosity to know what truth there was in all this, came to the door of the guest-chamber. But some time had elapsed since the nurse had given warning, and those two who had been overseen were sleeping in the shadow. The mother, gazing earnestly, thought to recognize the dress and the outline of the face. As she had no means of verifying what she saw she went back to bed: she counted on rising early and surprising her daughter, or, if too late, on learning all from Makhates, who could never lie when asked about such a matter. She retired, then, without saying anything. At the first light of day the young girl, whether at the beckoning of some god, or by chance, withdrew, and disappointed her mother. The latter came and was chagrined not to find her. Thereupon she told all she knew to the young man, her guest. She embraced the knees of Makhates, she adjured him to conceal nothing and not to distort the truth. He, touched, and anxious of heart, could scarcely speak.

"'Tis she, 'tis Philinnion," he said. And recounted how the union came about and the desires of the young girl who had said to him: "I hide from my parents in order to come to you." And that they might not doubt his words he opened a coffer and drew from it what she had left behind: a gold ring which he had had of her, and a strip of stuff that she had forgotten to knot round her bosom on the preceding night. Kharito, seeing these manifest signs, gave a loud cry, tore her garments, snatched the bands from her head, flung herself on the ground, and for the second time fell into great lamentation. Seeing everyone in the house in great grief and weeping, as though they must shortly

THE BRIDE OF CORINTH 83

bury Kharito, the guest, disturbed, set himself to console the mother, begged her to cease her laments, and promised to show her her daughter did she return. Kharito, moved by these words, was instant with him to be prompt in his promise, and returned to her dwelling. When night fell and the hour approached when Philinnion was used to come to the man she loved, all awaited her advent. She came. When she entered the chamber at the accustomed hour and when she was seated on the couch Makhates showed no surprise. He had no thought that he was consorting with a dead woman. The child had care to come to him at the time fixed; she ate and drank with him. He put no faith in what had been told to him. He supposed that someone among those whose business it was to bury the dead had taken from the sepulchre of Philinnion her garments and gold ornaments and had sold them to the father of the unknown girl who visited him. He sent a slave to summon Demostratos and Kharito. They came; they saw Philinnion. For the moment they stood dumb, overwhelmed, thunderstruck by such a prodigious sight. Then with loud outcry they embraced their daughter. Whereupon Philinnion said to them: "O father and mother mine, how unjustly do you grudge me the three days I may pass with this guest under the paternal roof, without undoing! Ye will weep afresh on account of your curiosity. As for me, I return to the habitation assigned me.

It was not without the divine will that I came hither." She spoke and fell dead. Her body reposed visibly on the bed. The father and mother embraced her. There was great tumult and lamentation throughout the household at a spectacle so terrible and irreparable, at so incredible a happening. The rumour of it spread quickly through the town and reached me. The same night I held back the crowd which flocked to the house, for I feared lest something extraordinary might be attempted on the making public of such tidings. That day the scene of events was crowded with the curious. When individual evidence had been taken of all the circumstances we agreed to go first of all to the tomb to satisfy ourselves if the corpse were in the coffin or whether it stood empty. When we had opened the vault where lay all the dead of this family we saw the other bodies stretched on their couch and the bones of those who had died long since. On the bed where Philinnion had been laid in her winding-sheet we found the guest's iron ring and the golden cup she had received on the first day from Makhates.

Surprised, surprised even to stupor, we went straightway to Demostratos and into the guest-chamber to see whether the body of the young girl were really there. Having seen it, stretched on the ground, we returned to the Assembly, for what had come about was a great and incredible thing. The Assembly being in a tumult, and as it was almost

THE BRIDE OF CORINTH

impossible to get anything done, Hyttos, who passes with us not only for an excellent divinator but also for a great augur, and who has deeply studied everything concerning the art of divination, rose and ordered that the corpse of the young girl should be inhumed outside the precincts (far from burying her a second time in the midst of us). He ordered that Hermes of the underworld and the Erinnys be appeased. He prescribed purification for each and all, that the sacred vessels be laved with lustral water and sacrifice offered to the gods of the dead. He particularly laid upon me that I sacrificed to the Emperor, to the Republic, to Hermes, to Zeus the Harbourer, and to Ares, and to do all with rigour. Thus he said, and we did what he ordained. Makhates, the guest whom the spectre had visited, killed himself in grief. In addition to this, if you decide that the Emperor must be made acquainted with this affair, let me know by letter. I could even send some witnesses who were spectators of all this. Farewell.

The author of this recital wished it to be believed to the letter, and he omits no circumstance which could give authenticity to the character of his tale. To be beforehand with the suspicious, he shows that he was himself of their number. And, in spite of the minute exactitude of the narrator, we are touched by something vague and deep-reaching in his tale. There is a beauty which escapes him in what he recounts. He sets out to describe a fact: he lets us perceive a symbol. The young girl, dead but amorous, somehow betrays her Christianity. The Nazarene has touched her youth. Goethe, whose genius lighted everything he looked into, illuminated the dark places of the Trallian. He made us see in these lovers, separated by their parents and re-united by some mysterious force, victims of the battle of the gods which shook the world from Nero's day to Constantine. He wrote *Die Braut von Korinth*.

I, in my turn, have taken up again and developed this old tale, for I have met nothing which better paints the decline of the gods of antiquity and the dawn of Christianity in a corner of Greece.

THE CHILD SOUL
(Âmes obscures)

UNCHANGING Nature's every trait
   Is marvel to the children, and
Their dim souls' unbidden way
   Breaks into wonderland.

The shining of its magic dawn
   Is caught and given in their glance ;
Their every sense, by beauty drawn,
   Trembles to utterance.

The Unknown assumes them, the Unknown,
   Deep waters of the abyss !
In vain you ask, insist—they own
   Another world than this.

Their limpid eyes, those grave wide eyes,
   Fill with the dreams they hold.
O children, out of Paradise,
   Lost in this world so old !

The lightly carried head and rapt
   Knows, not our mental strife,
But, thrill on thrill, and overlapt,
   The freshening waves of Life.

LIGHT
(À La Lumière)

From out the starry swarm's uncertain sheen
   Thou, the first-born, as of right,
Nurse of the flowers and of all fruits, O Light,
   White Mother of things seen

Down comest from the sun, 'cross softest bars
   Of aery vapour floating, still ;
Life stirs and wakes, and smiles to thy clear thrill,
   O daughter of the stars !

Hail ! For ere Thee were neither things nor days.
   Hail ! Sweetness and all might !
Hail ! Candid guide and giver of my sight,
   And keeper of my ways !

From Thee is colour, and all form divine,
   Thou shapest all we love ;
From Thee the glint on snow-peaks far above,—
   The valley's flushed decline.

Under blue skies thy jewelled birds rejoice
   In perfumes and in dews,
A grace on all things falls where fall thy hues,
   On all things of thy choice.

LIGHT

Joyous is morning for thy dear caress,
   The night thou leavest sweet
To woodland shadows, where in soft retreat
   Our lovers meet and press.

The deep sea's living blooms look up to heaven,
   Her sirens break in gold.
Thy rays entangled in the rain-drop's hold,
   Lend it the colours seven.

Thou lendest Woman all thy glorious guise,
   Light, 'tis Thou mak'st her fair !
And ever new the joy thy bounties spare
   From out her radiant eyes.

Her very ear shall make Thee throne to climb,
   And dazzle in a gem.
Where'er Thou shinest Thee will I acclaim,
   Virgin as at the prime.

Be Thou my strength, O Light, may my thought be
   Lucid and fair as Thou.
Thy grace and peace direct its forward flow,
   Still rhythmical with Thee.

Grant me to see until my days be told,
   Steeped in all joy and calm,
Beauty move queen-like over scattered palm,
   Crowned with Thy virgin gold.

LIGHT

When Nature to her breast resume what is,
   And shape her future dream,
Suffuse again, oh, lave with torrent stream,
   My metamorphosis!

THE DANCE OF DEATH
(*La Danse des Morts*)

In days of faith—when faith began to age—
The Dance of Death was oftentimes set out
Upon the charnel wall, or missal-page.

I think its edifying tale devout
Let in a little hope on deep despair;
That poor folk had as little fear as doubt.

Not that they looked to death to ease their care—
The devil grabs them once beneath the soil;
Hence from grey grief to utter dark they fare—

But that the master-painter, whose grave toil
Limned them this image, praying, on his knees,
Was monk, and breathed his peace on earthly broil.

Beneath the dancers' feet Hell's-mouth one sees,
Rattle of bones and live souls o'er the pit:
Grim :—but our Nothing did not menace these.

Sulphur enough—one gets the smell of it :—
And piteous to see abysmal darkness ope
For the poor suffering soul whose flesh is lit.

THE DANCE OF DEATH

Yet in this pictured story's ample scope
Speaks God's communion with each human soul;
One is aware of faith, and love, and hope.

Here is the mourning love that can console;
Sad are these dying, but make no complaint;
Death leads the flock nor uses hard control.

None breaks the ranks, they go with self-constraint,
They catch a wail of music, coaxing, thin,
Marking their step, moving with dolour faint.

Death goes before and plucks a mandolin,
And, wooer-like, that no man may him heed,
Hides his bowed ivory sconce his hat within.

Or, of his tribe, one holds a rustic reed
Against his white teeth grinning to the gaze,
Or strikes with bony hand the tabor's brede.

A female death of unaffected traits
Wakens the keyboard to her bony touch,
Even as St. Cecily, throned in a haze.

Their low-toned orchestra is scarcely such
As plays live men to church: it's quick'ning sound
Satan were wrong to envy overmuch.

For here, mark you, God's world may still be found,
Here Pope and Emperor still hold their sway,
And all the people led in peace profound.

THE DANCE OF DEATH

Great lords believe even as labourers may,
In all that David or the Sibyl sung ;
Their way is straight :—and horror lights the way.

But the Maid starts, and when, with arm loose-hung,
Her waist the Spectre circles, lover-wise,
Wakes to the touch her body fair and young.

Drooping her gaze before those hollow eyes,
Her wedding hymn she murmurs, closely prest,
For she is vowed to Bridegroom of the skies.

A marvellous dame rewards the Knightly quest.
Hangs on her open ribs, as on a grill,
A scrap of skin that once was woman's breast.

But he has vision of a woodland still,
His duchess riding in the month of May,
Whom he will see again :—God grant he will !

The Page, his youth's fair flower sere and grey,
Dances his road to Hell with steadfast mien.
Full well he knows his soul is damned alway.

The sightless Pedlar's steps had clumsy been,
But that Death, stepping soft with sober face,
Cuts the dog's cord with gentle hand unseen.

So groping towards the tinkle out of place
The blind man hies him to another night,
Not without many oaths :—God grant him grace !

Thus ends the dance and all are led aright.
Rufflers drop swords, the sceptred leave their throne;
Without complaint or noise so sleeps each wight

Expectant of the day his hound in stone,
At the stiff feet still couched in rigid care,
Wakes with wet tongue his master lying prone;

And judgment clarions through the dark shall blare,
Whose sound shall wake the echoes of his tomb
With tumult, and his bones shall be aware,

And dull cold Death, and Nature sick with gloom,
Shall see arise from every grave the form
Of every creature born of woman's womb.

All flesh of Adam won back from the worm;
And Death shall die: and void consume desire,
And worlds diverse Eternity inform.

Clad in the martyrs' white and shining guise,
Each spouse shall see, in nimbus of bright gold,
The well-beloved pass in white attire.

But they whose broken wings may ne'er unfold,
These, on the verge of burning sulphur-flood,
Shall suffer, yes: but still to life they hold.

THE DANCE OF DEATH

All tragic loves and widowed, marked with b
Drifting enlaced about their circle fell,
Shall sigh unceasing words now understood.

O happy they who yet believed in Hell!

Thy deep profound of soul, Thy gentle tone,
Gathered the women by the well-side way;
They poured their perfume on Thine hair; to-day
They light an aureole about Thine eyes,
God of the foolish virgin and the wise!
For ever shall be perfected in Thee
The fairest loves of men; 'tis Thy decree!
Each woman who weeps is Thine, in her distress;
Loosed from our jealous hold, each matted tress
Shall serve in turn to wipe Thy naked feet;
Slipped from our arms, from our relaxed entreat,
Till time be done, each Magdalen in turn
Pour at Thy waiting feet the plenished urn.
Christ! For Thy throne she leaves my soul to
    drouth,
To praise Thee with the honey of her mouth.

God's chalice, thou! My lips shall know the loss.
His mystic Rose, the Flower of the Cross!

GOOD-BYE
(*Adieu*)

I ENTERED in a church where depth of shade
Closed the drear day when veils of black are laid
O'er the gilt symbols of the saving rood
Whereon earth's debt to Heaven was made good.
A deacon, bowed, white-surpliced, and alone,
Watched at God's tomb, the shrouded altar-stone
Friday in Holy Week, when women come
To glide like shadows in the recessèd gloom;
On rustle of silk and jewels' silvern sound,
Roll Latin chant and organ-voice profound.
There I saw her to whom my life is lent
Kneel on her knees in soft abandonment,
Her head borne back with heavy weight of hair
And long hands on the velvet drooped, in prayer.
From out the darkling roof the lamps' spent light
Lit the cheek's inward curve of amorous white.
I was surprised to know her in that place
For her life's way was not God's path of grace.
I was beside her, touched her garments dark,
My shadow fell in hers, she did not mark.
What struck me was that, from her big eyes bright,
I ne'er had seen such brilliance of clear light.
I had not known such burning tears to lie

GOOD-BYE

On looks so lovely, such long ecstasy;
So sweet a tie, such thrill of fearful love,
Drew her to God, pale on the cross above.
So drank her sense the heavenly breath distilled,
The incense-fume wherewith the church was filled.

How prompt the woman-soul to spring on fire!
Her lips' red flower stood open in desire,
Her being throbbed to an unseen embrace;
So fear and sorrow took me for a space;
I saw henceforth her heart a citadel,
That she repented having loved too well;
That since God's fruitful grace had watered dearth,
Rose the disgust against the things of earth.
Then did I mourn myself, and was aware
That she had passed to Thee, O Jew too fair,
King with locks reddened by the thorny crown!

CRAINQUEBILLE
A PLAY IN THREE ACTS

To LUCIEN GUITRY

My dear Friend,

I make no offering of this little play to you. It is yours already. It is yours, not only because you gave it the hospitality of your theatre and staged it marvellously, and gave it with a picked caste; not merely because you yourself brought out the character of Crainquebille with astonishing power and masterly truth. It is yours because I should never have done it without your help, and because every scene that was received with favour was written entirely under your inspiration.

I inscribe your name on the front page of our Crainquebille in testimony of my friendship.

ANATOLE FRANCE

CHARACTERS

Crainquebille	Mm.	Guitry.
A Chestnut-vendor	,,	Francés.
The Magistrate, Bourriche	,,	Nertann.
Maître Lemerle	,,	Arquilliere.
Doctor David Mathieu	,,	Noizeux.
Aubarrée	,,	Fredal.
Police-Constable 64	,,	Talrick.
Lermite	,,	Larmandie.
A Street-hawker	,,	Favart.
A Grocer	,,	Laforest.
Police-constable 121	,,	Adam.
Usher	,,	Thoulouse.
A Wine-merchant	,,	Larry.
A Pork-butcher	,,	Mallet.
Madame Bayard	Mmes.	Marie Samary.
Madame Laura	,,	Irma Perrot.
The Mouse	,,	Juliette Margel.
A Work-girl	,,	Jane Beryl.
A Work-girl	,,	Jeanne Schmitt.

CRAINQUEBILLE

ACT I.

Rue de Beaujolais.

Scene I.

The Street-hawker.

(*Dressed like a shopwalker at the Magasins du Louvre, and standing on a stool, a box as big as a small trunk in front of him on a trestle, from which he keeps extracting articles that he as quickly replaces, he is just finishing his patter to the audience that crowds round him. Each time he mentions his firm's name he raises his tall hat.*)

. . . If the firm of Gameron, Cormandel & Co., which I have the honour to represent in this market-place, has at length decided to make the enormous sacrifices which I have just enumerated to you, it is not for purely humanitarian motives, gentlemen; don't you believe it. It is not the case, and I don't mind telling you so, that the firm of Gameron,

Cormandel & Co. has undertaken to ruin the large shops or even the small tradesmen, as some malicious people would vainly make you believe, by disseminating broadcast slanders that we only have to look full in the face to see sink beneath the ground. No, gentlemen, the firm of Gameron, Cormandel & Co. has kept its eye on one thing, one thing alone. It is rather an important thing, and I will tell you about it presently. I count on your well-known forbearance, and merely ask a moment's patience. I will profit by it to recapitulate : these six articles may be had by anyone who cares to ask for them ; he only has to say the word—a movement, a gesture, a mere wave of the hand, and they are his. These six articles, briefly enumerated, are as follows : First, a pneumatic cane which may be folded up by a mere pressure of the fingers, thus forming an object of small dimensions that will easily slip into an ordinary pocket. This article, in untarnishable metal, has a sale value of three shillings. I don't believe, gentlemen, you can accuse me of exaggeration. Think for one moment of the exorbitant price of labour nowadays. To continue: Secondly, a superb set of imitation shirt-studs. Three studs for the front, a pair of links for the cuffs, with detachable base, in burnished aluminium capable of resisting the action of fire for more than four hours. . . . Then the collar-stud, ornamented with a ravishingly beautiful blue stone, half a turquoise. I ask you all, gentlemen, and more

CRAINQUEBILLE

particularly those who are in this line of business, Do you think a jeweller?—and I am not referring to a Boucheron or a Vevers. I talk as one . . .

Scene II.

A Butcher's Boy
(*leaving the crowd, to the* Street-hawker).
You talk enough for two, guv'nor!

Street-hawker (*with a savage grin*).
Just you wait a bit, my young fellow. . . . Just half a minute . . . I shall have finished in a tick, I then shall be able to attend to you. . . .

The Butcher's Boy (*making a sign*).
Get up there, you will see Montmartre.
                                  [*He goes out.*

Scene III.

The Street-hawker (*continuing*).
You prefer to retire, young man; permission is given you. To continue: Is it likely, as I was saying, that a small jeweller, satisfied with a ridiculously small profit, could actually make this article under one-and-six? No. You agree? Well, I reckon one shilling, so far. Thirdly, a box of marvellous soap, the "Ocean Soap," of whose

wonderful qualities I gave you a conspicuous demonstration a few moments ago; it removes the most obstinate stains, and makes any material look as good as new. Gentlemen, I will not exhaust your powers of appreciation, and without saying any more about it, I offer it to you at the ridiculous figure of twopence-halfpenny. Fourthly, a box in Norwegian fire-bronzed celluloid, containing fifty pastilles, a certain remedy for all bronchial affections. Worth? What is it worth? A penny halfpenny. . . . Could anything be cheaper? Yes, and I will tell you what. This is the climax. The two remaining articles, the skirt-fastener, napkin-holder, automatic binder-clip, and, finally, the watch-chain, or a lady's necklace, very similar to gold. . . . The price? Nothing . . . chucked in. No shillings and no pence, which, added to the articles mentioned above, gives us a total of . . . (*rapidly*) Three shillings for the pneumatic cane, one for the imitation set, twopence halfpenny for the "Ocean Soap," three-ha'pence for the health-giving pastilles; four shillings and four pence, which the firm of Gameron, Cormandel & Co., whom I have the honour to represent here, have authorized me to make you a present of. Yes, I say a present; for I'm not asking four shillings and fourpence, nor three, two, or even one shilling—not even of sixpence. I'm merely asking, gentlemen, the nonsensical, the ridiculous, the amazing, the positively absurd sum of . . . twopence the lot (*they search their pockets*), and if, on your return to your homes, as you sit round the table in the light of the lamp when the evening meal is smoking on the board . . . if, prompted by a feeling of curiosity, and a quite excusable curiosity, gentlemen, you ask yourselves what has led the firm of Gameron, Cormandel & Co. to do this, stop right there in your investigations . . . give up trying to understand. . . . You will never succeed. . . . It is an advertisement!

[*He gives the articles to everyone who holds out his twopence, and the buyers examine them as they leave the stage.*

A Tradesman's Wife (*speaking to a workman*).
Is it any good, this stuff, for removing stains?

The Workman.
My good woman, I have been a cleaner and dyer for twenty-five years, haven't I? If it was any good I should use it . . . it's muck!

The Tradesman's Wife.
Anyway, it isn't dear at twopence, all this lot.

Crainquebille.
Cabbages! Carrots! Turnips!

Children (*returning from school*).
What ho, old daddy Crainquebille!

CRAINQUEBILLE.
Be off to school with you! instead of picking up bad ways in the streets. . . . But what else can they learn in the gutter? Nothing but bad . . . Any sparrowgrass!

A WOMAN.
Show us your asparagus.

LA SOURIS.
You ain't very bright. They're leeks, they are. Leeks is the poor man's 'sparagus . . . Everyone knows that. (*One of the little boys pulls about the bundles of leeks on the barrow.*) Just you leave that alone, he's got his living to earn. If you earned your bread as I do . . . you parcel of brats, you . . .

CRAINQUEBILLE.
Do you earn your living?

LA SOURIS.
I have to.

A CHILD.
'E ain't anybody. He sleeps out-of-doors. He's got no father or mother—they've left him.

CRAINQUEBILLE.
If 'e ain't got no parents, that's their fault, not his.

A Child.
He has nothing to eat and he keeps a dog! Why don't you eat your dog?

La Souris.
Who said I slept out-of-doors? Who said so? Say it again, that's all. I don't sleep out-of-doors—there's my bedroom window. . . .

A Child.
Your window hasn't got any glass in it. They are pulling down your house.

La Souris.
At night I mind that shop they are repairing. That shows that I am honest. And, anyway, you leave me alone!

Crainquebille.
What is your job?

La Souris.
I pick up fags, sell papers, run errands. Anything you like.

Crainquebille.
What's your name?

La Souris.
La Souris.

Crainquebille.
You are called La Souris? Well, you have more

sense than the rest of 'em. You know more about life.

LA SOURIS.

Because I have known what it is to be hungry. They—they don't know nothing. When you haven't been down on your luck your eyes aren't opened.

CRAINQUEBILLE.

You have known what it is to be without grub?

LA SOURIS.

Rather, and I know it still. That sort of thing sticks.

CRAINQUEBILLE.

Yes, you don't look very grand. Here, take this pear, it's a bit sleepy, but it's a good 'un—a William.

LA SOURIS.

It's quite soft. If your wife's heart is as tender! Thanks all the same, Crainquebille, old dad.

A LITTLE GIRL

(carrying a loaf bigger than herself, asks in a sing-song voice:)

Are your cabbages good?

CRAINQUEBILLE.

Couldn't be better. They are all heart.

THE LITTLE GIRL.
How much are they ? Mother's ill, and can't do her shopping herself.

CRAINQUEBILLE.
What is the matter with your mother ? What's she got ?

THE LITTLE GIRL.
I don't know. It's her inside. . . . She told me to buy a cabbage off you.

CRAINQUEBILLE.
Right 'o, don't be afraid, my little girl, I will serve you as well as if I'd been serving your mother. And better, for if I'd got to do anyone it would be a woman old enough to take care of herself. Oughtn't to do anyone, of course . . . everyone ought to get his money's worth. But if you couldn't help it I'd rather do someone who was trying to do the same to me. As to doing the dirty on a cherub like you, I should be sorry, and that's the truth. (*He gives her a cabbage.*) There, that's the finest I have. It's got a head like a Member of Parliament. (*The little girl gives him fourpence-halfpenny.*) Fivepence ! Another halfpenny, please. You ain't going to do *me* ?

THE LITTLE GIRL.
But mother only gave me fourpence-halfpenny.

CRAINQUEBILLE.
You mustn't tell stories, my dear. Look and see if you haven't got another halfpenny in your pocket.

THE LITTLE GIRL.
No, I only had fourpence-halfpenny.

CRAINQUEBILLE.
Well, my dear, give me a kiss, that will make it square, and you can ask your mother if the cabbage she found you in had as good a heart as this one. Run along, my dear, and mind you don't tumble. Good morning, Madame Laure, and how is the world treating you?

MADAME LAURE
(*yellow chignon, very juvenile*).
You've got nothing worth having, to-day.

CRAINQUEBILLE.
How can you say so?

MADAME LAURE (*tasting the radishes*).
Your radishes are all woolly.

CRAINQUEBILLE.
You must have woke up in a bad temper. This is your grumbling day.

MADAME LAURE.
They've got no taste in them. You might as well be eating water.

Crainquebille.

I tell you what it is : your taste is out of order—you don't know what you are eating. It's all through living in Paris. Your stomach gets burnt up. What would become of you all if old Crainquebille did not bring you fresh, cool vegetables. You would be on fire.

Madame Laure.

It isn't what I eat does me harm. I can only eat salad and radishes nowadays. Nevertheless, it's true you do get burnt up in Paris. (*Dreamily.*) Listen, Crainquebille, I should like to see the day when I could do without your cabbages and turnips, and grow them myself in a small garden eighty miles from Paris, at our home. It would be so peaceful in the country, rearing one's own pigs and poultry.

Crainquebille.

The day will come, Madame Laure, it will come : don't get downhearted. You're neat and thrifty, you're a sensible woman ; I do not busy myself about my customers' affairs. There are no bad trades, and there are good folk in all classes. But you are a sensible person. You will be rich when you get on in years, and you'll have a house of your own, a place of your own choosing, the place of your birth. . . . And you will be looked up to. Good-bye, Madame Laure.

MADAME LAURE.
Good-bye, daddy Crainquebille.

CRAINQUEBILLE.
What good folk there are in all walks of life! (*Shouting.*) Cabbages! Carrots! Turnips!

MADAME BAYARD (*issuing from her shop*).
I don't think much of your leeks. How much a bundle?

CRAINQUEBILLE.
Sevenpence-ha'penny, my good woman—best leeks going.

MADAME BAYARD.
Sevenpence-ha'penny for three bad leeks?

POLICE-CONSTABLE 64.
Move on, there!

CRAINQUEBILLE.
Yes—yes. They are yours. Hurry up, you heard the policeman.

MADAME BAYARD.
Well, but I must choose my stuff. Sevenpence-ha'penny! No fear! Will you take sixpence?

CRAINQUEBILLE.
They cost me more than that, my little lady. And then I have to be at the market at five o'clock and even earlier if I want anything good.

Constable 64.

Move on, there!

Crainquebille.

Yes, yes, in a minute. Here, hurry up, Madame Bayard.

Madame Bayard.

Sixpence.

Crainquebille.

And ever since seven o'clock this morning I've been blistering my hands on these shafts shouting "Cabbages! Turnips! Carrots!" and all so much waste of time and money. At past sixty, you will understand, I don't do it for fun. Oh, no, it's not good enough. Why, I shouldn't make a penny on it.

Madame Bayard.

I will give you sevenpence. And I must go in and get it from the shop, for I haven't got it on me. [*She goes in.*

Constable 64.

Move on!

Crainquebille.

I am waiting for my money.

Constable 64.

I didn't tell you to wait for your money. I told you to move on.... Well? What, don't you know what " move on " means?

CRAINQUEBILLE.
For fifty years I have known it, and pushed my cart. . . . But they owe me money there at "The Guardian Angel," Madame Bayard's boot-shop. She's gone to look for sevenpence for me, and I am waiting.

CONSTABLE 64.
Do you want me to summons you? Do you? Get along. Clear the road. D'you hear?

CRAINQUEBILLE.
Good God! for fifty years I have earned my bread selling cabbages, leeks, and turnips, and because I do not want to lose sevenpence owing me . . .
[*A butcher's boy stops.*

CONSTABLE 64
(*pulling out his pencil and notebook*).
Show me your licence.

CRAINQUEBILLE.
My licence?

CONSTABLE 64.
Yes, your hawker's licence.
[*Enter a pastrycook's boy.*

CRAINQUEBILLE.
Look here, old pal, if you want to see my licence you must come home with me.

CRAINQUEBILLE

CONSTABLE 64.

You haven't got a licence ?

CRAINQUEBILLE.

Yes, I've got one, but it's at home. I've lost three by carrying 'em about with me. That cost me three shillings each time, so I gave it up.

CONSTABLE 64.

Your name ?

CRAINQUEBILLE.

Oh, rot ! I suppose I've got to lose my sevenpence, that's all.

[*He takes hold of his cart and pushes on.*

CONSTABLE 64.

Stop, will you ?

CRAINQUEBILLE.

I am off . . .

CONSTABLE 64.

No, you're not, it's too late.

[*He advances on* CRAINQUEBILLE, *and takes him by the arm;* CRAINQUEBILLE *turns round just in time to receive a whole load of rubbish on his barrow from the house-breakers, who curse and swear at him.*

THE HOUSE-BREAKERS.

God love us ! Look at that barrow !

Constable 64.

Look what you've done.

[*A newsvendor on a bicycle runs full tilt into the off side of* Crainquebille's *barrow. He yells.*

The Newsvendor

(*with a hundred and fifty copies of "La Patrie" on his head*).

Look where you're going, you stupid old turnip-head!

Constable 64.

You see? You see?

[*He goes to the right of* Crainquebille *who, turning completely round, manages to jamb his left wheel into the left wheel of a cart bearing a copper bath, and drawn by a man who starts cursing and swearing.*

Oh, you've done it this time!

Crainquebille.

Hallo! Now, how are you going to move on?

Constable 64.

This is all your fault.

Crainquebille.

The whole fault is Madame Bayard's. If she was here she'd say so. Funny she isn't here. Where has she hidden herself? Looking for her coppers.

CRAINQUEBILLE

[*Meanwhile, street-urchins, workmen, shop-people, idlers, all sorts of people appear; from the background, in the wake of the house-breaker's cart, a van laden with boxes filled with syphons comes on the scene; a dog jumps about on the top of the boxes, barking furiously. Slowly the van merges into the heap of conveyances, and contributes its share to the conglomeration of vehicles. Sixty people cover the footpath, the road, the steps, the carriages, thirty lean out of the windows. All these folk move about and gesticulate. The constable loses his head, claps* CRAINQUEBILLE *on the shoulder and says:*

Constable 64.

Oh, so you said "Bloody copper!" did you? All right. You come with me.

Crainquebille.

I said that—I? I never!

Constable 64.

Yes, you said it.

Crainquebille.

"Bloody copper"?

[*Laughter.*

Constable 64.

Ah, and what about that then?

CRAINQUEBILLE.
What?

CONSTABLE 64.
You didn't say " bloody copper "?   [*Laughter.*

CRAINQUEBILLE.
Yes.

CONSTABLE 64.
Ah!

CRAINQUEBILLE.
But I did not say it to you.   [*Laughter.*

CONSTABLE 64.
You did not say it?

CRAINQUEBILLE.
But, Gor blimey!

A MAN.
What is the matter?

CRAINQUEBILLE.
The matter is, he says I turned and called him a (*he turns again to the constable and calls out to demonstrate*) " bloody copper! "

CONSTABLE 64
(*who is taking notes in his book, gets this full in the face, and observes quite calmly*):
Oh, now you may say it a hundred times; there's no extra charge.

Crainquebille.
But I am explaining to them.

A Man (*to another, smiling*).
It doesn't matter a blow to me, but he said it at least three times.

Another Man.
No, it was the policeman who made him say it.

The Man.
Oh, no, I am certain the policeman would not have done that.

Another Bystander.
He saw everyone laughing, and he was annoyed, and he lost his head.

Crainquebille.
Nevertheless, it is all very simple. . . .

Constable 64.
Here, that'll do!

[*He seizes* Crainquebille. *A white-haired old man,* Dr. David Mathieu, *comes up; he is in black, wears a tall hat, and is decorated with the rosette of the Legion of Honour.*

Dr. Mathieu
(*gently pulling the policeman by his sleeve*).
Allow me, allow me. You have made a mistake.

CONSTABLE 64.
Mistake, eh! What's that?

DR. MATHIEU (*firmly and gently*).
You misunderstood. This man did not insult you.

CONSTABLE 64.
Misunderstood?

DR. MATHIEU.
I witnessed the whole scene, and I heard all that was said perfectly well.

CONSTABLE 64.
Well?

DR. MATHIEU.
And I assure you this man said nothing to cause . . .

CONSTABLE 64.
Mind your own business.

DR. MATHIEU.
I ask your pardon. It is my right, my duty, to warn you of an error that might have grievous consequences for this good man, and it is my right and duty to bear witness . . .

CONSTABLE 64.
You keep a civil tongue in your head.

A Workman.

The gentleman is right—the costermonger did not say " bloody copper."

The Crowd.

Yes! Yes, he did say it. No! Yes! Oh! Come! I say, look here!

Constable 64 (*to the workman*).

You want to be run in, I suppose?
                    [*The workman disappears.*

Dr. Mathieu (*to* Constable 64).

You have not been insulted. The words you thought you heard were never uttered. When you are calmer you will acknowledge it yourself.

Constable 64.

To begin with, who are you? I do not know you.

Dr. Mathieu.

Here is my card. Dr. Mathieu, senior surgeon at the Ambroise Paré Hospital.

Constable 64.

I don't care for that.

Dr. Mathieu.

But you must care. I shall be obliged if you

will take my name and address, and make a note of what I say.

Constable 64.

Oh, so you insist! Well then, come with me. You can explain the matter to the inspector.

Dr. Mathieu.

That is just my intention.

A Working-woman
(*to her husband, pointing to the* Doctor).

It's queer—a well-dressed man, well educated—and he mixes himself up with this affair. . . . If it proves disagreeable for him it is his own fault. Never mix yourself up in other folk's affairs. Come, let's be off, my dear. I quite saw how it all happened: he was calling Madame Bayard, saying, "Where is she with her coppers," and the policeman thought he heard "bloody coppers." Come on, come on, or you will be called as a witness.

Madame Bayard (*coming out of her shop*).

Here's your money. . . . Why, he's been arrested. I can't give money to a man who has been taken up. One can't do that. I am not sure that it would be allowed.

[*The crowd has played a great part in all this in a series of considerable movements of uncertain tendency. The rabble now press close on the heels of the little group formed by* Police-

CONSTABLE 64, CRAINQUEBILLE, *and the elderly gentleman. There is a frightful uproar; oaths, laughter, cries of street-boys, bicycle-horns, barking dogs, and the yells of a child that is being spanked by its mother, and countless other noises are heard, now singly, now together.*

ACT II.

A room in the Police Court.

THE MAGISTRATE, BOURRICHE
(reading his judgment).
The Court, after due deliberation, according to law, holds that, whereas . . .

THE USHER.

Silence!

THE MAGISTRATE.

. . . it sufficiently appears from the documents put in evidence and from the depositions heard at the last hearing, that on October 3 Fromage (Alexandre) was found guilty of the offence of mendicity, an offence provided for and punished by Article 274 of the Penal Code. The said Article condemns Fromage (Alexandre) to six days' imprisonment. (FROMAGE, *who had been seated by*

Crainquebille's *side, is led away by two warders. An interval.* ... *Some noise.* ... *The magistrate turns over his papers.*) Your name is Crainquebille. Stand up. Your name is Crainquebille (Jérôme), born at Poissy (Seine) on July 14, 1843. You have never been previously convicted.

Crainquebille.

Ask me what you like. I owe nothing to anyone. That I can say. A halfpenny is a halfpenny to me. I am never out in my dealings.

The Magistrate.

Keep silence. At midday, on July 25 last, in the Rue de Beaujolais, you insulted and abused a constable in the exercise of his duty. You applied to him the words " b— copper " (*he only pronounces the first letter*). You acknowledge the facts ?

Crainquebille
(*turning towards his lawyer*).
What does he say ? Is he speaking to me ?

The Magistrate.

You used threats ; you called out " b— copper " (*he only promounces the first letter*).

Crainquebille.

" Bloody copper," you mean.

THE MAGISTRATE.
You do not deny it ?

CRAINQUEBILLE.
On all that I hold most sacred—on my daughter's head if I had one—I did not insult the policeman. To that I take my Bible oath.

THE MAGISTRATE.
Let us have your version of the affair. Reconstitute the scene.

CRAINQUEBILLE.
Your worship, I am an honest man ; I owe nobody anything. I know the value of a halfpenny. I deal squarely with all, I can say that. For forty years I've been known in the market in Montmartre and everywhere. I used to earn my living when I was only fourteen . . .

THE MAGISTRATE.
I did not ask for your biography. [*Stir in Court.*

THE USHER.
Silence !

THE MAGISTRATE.
I ask you to give your version of what occurred during the scene preceding your arrest.

CRAINQUEBILLE.

All I can tell you is that for forty years, ever since I have pushed my barrow, I have known what the police are. As soon as I see one coming, off I slope. And so I have never had any difficulty with them. But as to insulting them, by word, or in any other way, never! that has never been my way. Why should I be supposed to change at my age?

THE MAGISTRATE.

You resisted the constable's orders, when he told you to move on.

CRAINQUEBILLE.

Oh, come! Move on, indeed! If you could have seen. Why, the carts were all jammed into one another so, it was not even possible to move a wheel.

THE MAGISTRATE.

Well, do you acknowledge having said " b— copper "?

CRAINQUEBILLE.

I said " bloody copper " because the officer said " bloody copper." So I said " bloody copper." You see?

THE MAGISTRATE.

Do you ask me to believe that the constable used this expression first?

CRAINQUEBILLE
(*in despair of making himself understood*).
I don't ask you to believe anything. I . . .

THE MAGISTRATE.
You do not persist. Quite right. You may sit down.   [*An interval. Stir in Court.*

THE USHER.
Silence!

THE MAGISTRATE.
We will hear the evidence. Usher, call the first witness.

THE USHER
(*leaving the Court, makes his way through the crowd, calling out*).
Police-constable Bastien Matra.
              [*Enter* MATRA, *wearing his belt.*

THE MAGISTRATE.
Your name, age, and occupation.

MATRA.
Matra (Bastien), born August 15, 1870, in Bastia (Corsica). Police-constable No. 64.

THE MAGISTRATE.
You swear to speak the truth, the whole truth, and nothing but the truth. Say, "I swear."

MATRA.
I swear.
THE MAGISTRATE.
Give your evidence.

MATRA (*unfastening his belt*).
While on duty on October 20 at midday I noticed a person in the Rue Beaujolais who seemed to be a street-hawker, and who had drawn up his barrow for an undue length of time opposite No. 28, causing a block in the traffic. I told him three times to move on, which he refused to do. And on my warning him that I should report him, he answered me by exclaiming " bloody copper," which seemed to me to be insulting language.

THE MAGISTRATE
(*in a fatherly tone to* CRAINQUEBILLE).
You hear what the constable says.

CRAINQUEBILLE.
I said " bloody copper " because he said " bloody copper." So then *I* said " bloody copper." It is quite easy to see that.

THE MAGISTRATE
(*who has not been listening, and who is preparing to pass judgment*).
There are no other witnesses ?

THE USHER.
Yes, your worship, there are two more.

THE MAGISTRATE.
What ? Two more ?

LEMERLE.
We have subpœnaed two witnesses for the defence.

THE MAGISTRATE.
Do you wish them to be heard, Monsieur Lemerle ?

LEMERLE.
Yes, certainly, your worship.

THE MAGISTRATE
(*sighing, to the constable, who is buckling on his belt again*).
Let the constable remain.

THE USHER (*calling*).
Madame Bayard.
[*Enter* MADAME BAYARD *in her best clothes.*

THE MAGISTRATE.
Your name, age, and occupation.

MADAME BAYARD.
Pauline Felicité Bayard, keeper of a boot shop at No. 28 Rue Beaujolais.

THE MAGISTRATE.

What age are you?

MADAME BAYARD.

Thirty. [*Stir in Court.*

THE USHER.

Silence!

THE MAGISTRATE.

Swear to speak the truth, the whole truth, nothing but the truth. Raise your hand and say, "I swear." (MADAME BAYARD *raises her hand.*) Take the glove off your right hand. . . . Usher, make her withdraw her glove. . . . (*She takes off her glove.*) Say, "I swear."

MADAME BAYARD.

I swear.

CRAINQUEBILLE.

She does not seem to recognize me. She is too stuck up.

THE USHER.

Silence!

THE MAGISTRATE (*to* MADAME BAYARD).

Tell us what you have to say. (MADAME BAYARD *is silent.*) Tell us what you know of the scene which took place before Crainquebille's arrest.

MADAME BAYARD (*in a low voice*).
I was buying a bundle of leeks, and the dealer said to me, "Hurry up." I replied ...

THE MAGISTRATE.
Speak distinctly.

MADAME BAYARD.
I answered that, all the same, I must pick and choose. At that moment a customer entered the shop, and I went to serve her. It was a lady with a child.

THE MAGISTRATE.
Is that all you have to say?

MADAME BAYARD.
While the coster was having words with the policeman I was trying some blue shoes on a child of eighteen months; I was trying him on blue shoes ...

THE MAGISTRATE (*to* LEMERLE).
Counsel, have you any questions to put to this witness? (LEMERLE *makes a sign in the negative*.) And you, Crainquebille? Have you any question to put to the witness?

CRAINQUEBILLE.
Yes. I have a question to put.

The Magistrate.
Put it.

Crainquebille.
I have to ask Madame Bayard whether she heard me say " bloody copper." She knows me. She is one of my customers. She can tell you if it is like me to use words like that. (MADAME BAYARD *remains silent.*) You can speak for me, Madame Bayard; you are an old customer of mine.

The Magistrate.
Do not address the witness. Address yourself to the Court.

Crainquebille
(*who does not understand these subtleties*).
Come, Madame Bayard, we know one another. Proof of it is that you still owe me sevenpence. I don't ask you for it now. I am above caring about sevenpence, thank God.   [*Laughter and noise.*

The Usher.
Silence!

Crainquebille.
But I want them to know that you are a customer.

Madame Bayard
(*to* CRAINQUEBILLE *as she leaves the Court*).
I do not know you.

THE MAGISTRATE (*to the witness*).

You may retire. (*To* LEMERLE.) This evidence does not in any way contradict the constable's. Is there still another witness ?

LEMERLE.

One only.

THE MAGISTRATE.

Do you insist on his being heard by the Court ?

LEMERLE.

Your worship, I consider that the evidence you are about to hear is necessary for the demonstration of the truth. It is that of an eminent man, whose deposition is, to my thinking, important, essential, and decisive.

THE MAGISTRATE (*with an air of resignation*).
Call the last witness.

THE USHER.

Dr. Mathieu. [*Enter* DR. MATHIEU.

THE MAGISTRATE.

Your name, age, and profession.

DR. MATHIEU.

Mathieu (Pierre Philippe David), sixty-two years of age, senior surgeon at the Ambroise Paré Hospital, officer of the Legion of Honour.

THE MAGISTRATE.

Swear to speak the truth, the whole truth, nothing but the truth. Raise your hand and say, " I swear."

DR. MATHIEU.

I swear.

THE MAGISTRATE (*to* LEMERLE).

Counsel, what question do you wish put to the witness ?

LEMERLE.

Dr. Mathieu was present at the time of Crainquebille's arrest. I beg of your worship, that he be asked what he saw and what he heard.

THE MAGISTRATE.

You have heard the question ?

DR. MATHIEU.

I found myself in the crowd that had collected round the police-constable who was ordering this costermonger to move on. The crush was such that it was impossible to move. So I became a witness of the scene which took place, and I can affirm that I did not lose a word of it. It was perfectly plain to me that the constable was mistaken ; he was never insulted. The costermonger did not say what the constable thought he heard. My observation was corroborated by the people round me, who were unanimous in confirming the error. I went up to the constable, and warned him of his mistake. I drew his attention to the fact that this man had never insulted him, that, on the contrary, he had been very restrained in his language. The constable had him under arrest, and invited me somewhat roughly to follow him to the Court of Inquiry, which I did. I repeated my statement before the inspector.

THE MAGISTRATE (*icily*).
Good. You may sit down. Matra... (MATRA, *having put down his belt, the object of his solicitude, enters the box.*) Matra, when you proceeded to arrest the accused, did not Dr. Mathieu call your attention to the fact that you were mistaken? (*Silence on the part of* MATRA.) You have just heard Dr. Mathieu's evidence. I ask you, if, when you proceeded to arrest Crainquebille, did not Dr. Mathieu give you to understand that he believed you to be mistaken?

MATRA.
Mistaken? Mistaken? That is to say, your worship, he insulted me.

THE MAGISTRATE.
What did he say to you?

MATRA.
Why, he said, " bloody copper "—just like that.

THE MAGISTRATE (*hurriedly*).
You may retire.
[*While* MATRA *refastens his belt there is a buzz of talk, and uproar, and a look of pained astonishment on* DR. MATHIEU'S *pale face.*

LEMERLE
(*waving his sleeves amid the din*).
I leave the witness's evidence with confidence to the judgment of the Court.   [*The din continues.*

A VOICE IN THE COURT (*heard amid the bubbub.*)
He has got a smack in the eye, the bobby. You will get off, Crainquebille, old boy!

THE USHER.
Silence!   [*Order is gradually restored.*

THE MAGISTRATE.
These demonstrations are grossly improper. If they occur again I shall have the Court cleared immediately. Monsieur Lemerle, I will hear you now. (*Counsel unfolds his brief.*) Shall you be long?

LEMERLE.
No; it seems to me that the evidence given by the constable has singularly shortened my speech for the defence, and if this feeling is shared by the Court, I . . .

THE MAGISTRATE (*very sharply*).
I asked you if you would be long.

LEMERLE.
Twenty minutes at most.

THE MAGISTRATE (*resigned*).
I will hear you.

LEMERLE.
Gentlemen, I appreciate, I esteem, and I respect the executive of the law. An incident in Court, however characteristic it may be, cannot make me swerve from the favourable opinion I have of these modest servants of society, who, gaining but a mere pittance in the way of salary, endure fatigue and risk unceasing danger, and practise that daily heroism which is, perhaps, the most difficult of all. They are old soldiers, they remain soldiers ...

VOICE (*from amid the crowd*).
There he goes, pleading for the coppers. Why don't you defend Crainquebille? Coward!
[*An officer turns one of the public out of Court.*

THE VICTIM.
I tell you I said nothing. I tell you I never said a word!

LEMERLE (*continuing*).
No, I do not fail to acknowledge the valuable and

unvaunted services rendered daily by the guardians of the law to the good citizens of Paris. And I should not have consented, gentlemen, to address you in defence of Crainquebille had I seen in him a man capable of insulting an old soldier. Let us look at the facts. My client is accused of having spoken the words "bloody copper." What have we here—the national adjective, as it has been called, and a noun derived from the verb " cop," meaning to catch or take. We have here, gentlemen, quite a curious little study in popular philology. If you open a slang dictionary you will read (*he reads*): "Bloody, a corruption of 'By our Lady'"; "Copper, a slang word for policeman, from 'cop,' to catch or take." "Bloody copper" is an expression used by a certain class of people. But the whole question is this: In what spirit did Crainquebille say it, or rather, did he say it at all? Allow me, gentlemen, to have my doubts. I do not suspect Constable Matra of any ill-intention. But his, as we have said, is a wearisome task. Sometimes he is tired, overworked, overstrained. In these conditions he may well be the victim of a kind of hallucination of the mind. And when it comes to his telling us that Dr. Mathieu, officer of the Legion of Honour, senior surgeon at the Ambroise Paré Hospital, a light of science and a man of the world, called out " bloody copper," we are, indeed, forced to the conclusion that Matra is a prey to the malady of obsession, and, if the term is not too strong, to a frenzied delusion of persecution.

Voices from the Court
(*manifold and exuberant expressions of approbation*).

Yes! Indeed! Yes! Say no more! it is plain enough! Good! Good!

The Usher.
Silence!

The Magistrate.
All marks of approval or disapproval being strictly forbidden, I shall order the officers to clear the Court of all disturbers.

[*Silence as of the grave.*

Lemerle.
Gentlemen, I have here before me a book that is an authority on the subject, "A Treatise on Hallucinations," by Brierre de Boismont, Doctor of Medicine of Paris, Knight of the Legion of Honour, of the Military Order of Poland, etc. One learns therein that hallucinations of the auditory sense are frequent, very frequent, and that people quite sound mentally may suffer from them under the influence of violent emotion, of excessive fatigue, of mental or physical overstrain. And what is the usual, the most common form of these hallucinations of the auditory sense? What words did Constable Matra think he heard in this unusual condition, caused by mistaken aural perceptions?

Dr. Brierre de Boismont will tell us. (*He reads.*) " For the most part, these delusions are connected with the preoccupations, habits, and passions of the patient." Take note, gentlemen, with the preoccupations, habits. Thus, during this period of hallucination, the surgeon hears the cries of his patients; the broker, the quotations on the Stock Exchange; the politician, the angry questions of his fellow-legislators; the police-officer, the cry of " bloody copper." Is it necessary to dwell upon it, gentlemen? (*A sign in the negative from the magistrate.*) And even if Crainquebille did call out " bloody copper," it remains to be seen whether the words on his lips bear a criminal interpretation. Gentlemen, on the question of breaking the law, it suffices that the infraction should be proved, the good or bad faith of the offender matters little. (*Buzz of talk.*) But here we are before the Penal Code. It is a question of equity. What the Court proceeds against, what you punish, gentlemen, is the wrongful intention. Before a criminal Court the intention becomes the essential element of the crime. Well, in this matter did the intention exist? No, gentlemen. [*Noise grows louder.*

THE USHER.

Silence!

LEMERLE.

Crainquebille is the illegitimate child of an itinerant market-woman, brought very low by drink and evil living. He . . .

A Voice in the Crowd.
He is insulting his mother now.

Lemerle.
. . . was born an alcoholic, of a naturally limited intelligence; uneducated, he has merely instincts. And if you will allow me to say so, those instincts are not fundamentally evil, but they are brutish. His soul is embedded in a thick matrix. He has no exact understanding of what is said to him, nor of what he himself says. Words have but a rudimentary and confused meaning for him. He is one of those miserable beings whom La Bruyère depicts in such sombre colours, men one might take for brute beasts, they so grovel on the earth. You see him before you, brutalized by sixty years of grinding poverty. Gentlemen, you may well say that he is irresponsible.

The Magistrate.
The Court will now consider its judgment.
[*Noise. The two coadjutors lean over the magistrate, who whispers.*

Crainquebille (*to his counsel*).
You must have some book-learning to talk like that, right off the reel, too. You speak well, but

you speak too quickly. People cannot understand anything you say. Me, for instance, I don't know what you have been talking about, but I am grateful all the same ; only . . .

The Usher.
Silence !

Crainquebille.
It gives me a pain in my belly to hear him call out, that chap. . . . Only you ought to have mentioned that I owe no one anything. Because it's true. I am an honest man. I owe no one a farthing. After all, perhaps you did . . . perhaps you did mention it, and I did not hear. . . . And then, you ought to have asked them what they did with my barrow . . .

Lemerle.
In your own interest, be quiet.

Crainquebille.
Are they cackling over my sentence all this time ? Well, they are a long time about it, God knows . . .

The Usher.
Silence ! [*Silence reigns.*

The Magistrate
(*reading from a pile of papers—notices of deaths, marriages, prospectuses, etc*).
The Court . . .

A Voice

(*from the crowd, bursting upon the silence*).
Acquits! . . .

The Magistrate (*with a look of thunder*).
. . . after deliberation, according to the law, taking into consideration the result of the documents in the case, and of the evidence heard in this Court, finds that on July 25, the day of his arrest, Crainquebille (Jérôme) committed the offence . . . (*a dull and formidable murmur rises from the back of the Court; the magistrate greets this murmur with a glance like a sword-edge, and continues to read amid sudden silence*) . . . of outrage against a member of the public force, in the exercise of his duty, an offence provided for and punishable under Article 224 of the Penal Code. In terms of the aforesaid Article he is therefore condemned to fourteen days' imprisonment and a fine of *forty shillings*. The sitting is suspended. [*Uproar.*

Several Voices.
It is a bit stiff, all the same. . . . I should not have expected that. . . . It's a bit thick, that.

Crainquebille (*to the warder*).
So I am found guilty?
[*The Court retires. When the warders are about to remove* Crainquebille, Lemerle *indicates that he has something to say, and sorting his papers, he talks, etc.*

Scene II.

CRAINQUEBILLE (*to the warder*).

I say! You! I say! Who'd have thought a fortnight ago this would happen to me. They are very polite, these gentlemen. They don't use bad language, to give them their due, but you can't explain things to them. There isn't time. It isn't their fault, but you don't get time, do you? Why don't you answer? (*Silence.*) Can't you throw a word to a dog? Why don't you speak? Can't you open your mouth? Does your breath stink?

LEMERLE (*to* CRAINQUEBILLE).

Well, my friend, we have not much to complain about. We might have come off worse.

CRAINQUEBILLE.

That's true, too.

LEMERLE.

What do you expect? You would not take my advice. Your reticent method was unfortunate to a degree. You would have done better to confess.

CRAINQUEBILLE.

I would have done so right enough, my lad. But what should I have confessed? (*Pensively.*) Anyhow, it's an odd thing to happen to me.

Lemerle.

We must not make too much of it. Your case is not unusual—far from it. . . . Come, cheer up!

Crainquebille

(*as the warders take him away, turns back and says*).

You can't tell me what they have done with my barrow?

Aubarrée.

What are you doing there?

Lermite.

I am finishing my sketch. During the sitting I am forced to draw inside my hat. It is most inconvenient. So now I am adding a touch or two.

Aubarrée.

Is that Bourriche, the magistrate, you have got there?

Lermite.

Was it he who just sentenced the costermonger?

Aubarrée.

Yes, Bourriche!

Lermite.

Queer that that should be the case.

Lemerle (*to the* Usher).

Lamperière, do you know if the Goupy case in the Third Court has been adjourned?

The Usher.

It is on now.

Lemerle.

Blazes! I must fly! I will return shortly, when the Court sits again. I have to ask Bourriche to postpone a case.

Lermite

(*shyly, and feeling awkwardly in his pocket, calls to* Lemerle, *who does not hear him, but goes out*).

Monsieur Lemerle, I should like to have a word with you. There, he has gone!

Aubarrée.

He will be here again when the Court resumes the sitting. What do you want to say to him?

Lermite.

Nothing . . . I . . . Nothing. I say, old boy, that poor costermonger's sentence was a bit hard, all the same.

Aubarrée.

Crainquebille's? It *is* hard, I dare say. Yet it is not exceptionally hard. (*Looking over his shoulder.*) Are you going to make a picture out of that sketch?

Lermite.

Yes. Scenes in Court are in fairly good demand. This morning I sold two barristers for a fiver. I have the note in my pocket.

Aubarrée.
You need not flourish it like that.

Lermite.
Say what you like, Aubarrée, the magistrate sentenced that poor man without proof . . .

Aubarrée.
Without proof?

Lermite.
Treating Dr. David Mathieu's declaration with contempt . . . on the constable's evidence alone; it is beyond me, quite beyond my understanding.

Aubarrée.
Nevertheless, it is quite easy to understand.

Lermite.
What, to lend ear to the braying of that ignoble, dull, obstinate creature, rather than to the disinterested evidence of a man of outstanding merit and the highest intelligence. To believe the ass before the wise man—you think that natural? Do you? Why, it is monstrous! This magistrate Bourriche is a sinister kind of joker.

Aubarrée.
Don't say that, Lermite, don't say that. Bourriche is a respected magistrate who has just given us fresh proof of his judicial mind.

LERMITE.
In the Crainquebille affair?

AUBARRÉE.
Certainly. By weighing one against the other the contradictory attestations of Police-constable 64 and of Professor David Mathieu, the judge would have committed himself to a line of conduct where only uncertainty and doubt are to be met with. Bourriche has too judicial a mind to base his sentences on science and reason, whose conclusions are subject to never-ending dispute.

LERMITE.
So a judge must renounce knowledge?

AUBARRÉE.
Yes, but he must not renounce giving judgment. The fact of the matter is, Bourriche does not take Bastien Matra into consideration. He considers Police-constable 64. Man is fallible, he reflects. Descartes and Gassendi, Leibnitz and Newton, Claude Bernard and Pasteur, were all liable to mistake. But Police-constable 64 makes no mistake. He is merely a number. A number is not subject to error.

LERMITE.
Well, we'll call that an argument.

Aubarrée.
An irrefutable one. And then there is something else. Police-constable 64 is the strong arm of the State. All the weapons of a State should point the same way. By opposing them, one against the other . . .

Lermite.
Public peace is disturbed. I understand.

Aubarrée.
And, finally, if the Court decides against the executive, who would carry out its judgments? Without the police the judge would be but a sorry dreamer of dreams. [*Enter* Lemerle.

Lemerle.
Aubarrée, you are wanted in Court Four. Why! hasn't the Court resumed yet?

Aubarrée.
No.

Lemerle.
Isn't the usher here?

Lermite.
Excuse me, sir. . . . Does the infliction of a fine entail in case of non-payment a prolongation of imprisonment?

Lemerle.
Yes.

LERMITE.

Then would you be kind enough to give these two sovereigns to your costermonger?

LEMERLE.

Crainquebille?

LERMITE.

Yes, without telling him whom the money comes from.

LEMERLE.

Willingly, monsieur.

LERMITE.

But I must ask change for a fiver.

LEMERLE (*searching his pocket*).

Let me see . . . perhaps I . . . no, three pounds; oh, yes, here are ten shillings, fifty and ten, sixty. There, monsieur.

LERMITE.

Thank you.

LEMERLE.

It is I who thank you in his name.

DR. MATHIEU (*to* LEMERLE).

You were Crainquebille's counsel, were you not, sir? I have been looking for you.

LEMERLE.

Oh, yes! You are Dr. David Mathieu. You gave evidence for us.

DR. MATHIEU.

Could you give these two sovereigns to your client to pay his fine?

LEMERLE.

With the greatest pleasure. But I have already received two pounds from this gentleman (*pointing to* LERMITE) for the same object.

DR. MATHIEU.

Ah . . . [*Bows. Silence.*

LEMERLE

(*holding in each hand two pounds—two from* LERMITE *and two from the doctor*).

What do you propose, gentlemen?

DR. MATHIEU.

Well . . . two pounds for the fine.

LERMITE.

Yes, and two when he comes out.

LEMERLE.

Very good. You may count on me, gentlemen.
   [*He bows and goes out. Short silence.*

MATHIEU *and* LERMITE *bow in a friendly way.* MATHIEU *turns to go, followed, a few steps behind, by* LERMITE. MATHIEU *stops almost on the threshold, and turns back to* LERMITE, *who is close to him. The two men, with hands outstretched, say in unison:* "*Will you allow me?*" . . . *They smile and shake each other warmly by the hand, not without a touch of melancholy.* MATHIEU *goes out.*

THE USHER *announces the Court.*

LERMITE.

Here goes again.

ACT III

Night.

SCENE I.

THE CHESTNUT-VENDOR.

Chestnuts all hot!
[*He wraps up a ha'porth for a small boy.*

Crainquebille

(*coming out of a wine-shop where he has been having words*).

Well, what of it? Because I ask for a glass on tick. Is that any reason to treat me like a pickpocket?

The Chestnut-vendor.

Credit is dead, the debtors have killed it.

Crainquebille.

I ask anyone, couldn't he have trusted me for a glass? He got plenty out of me while I had anything. You are a thief, and I tell you so straight.

The Chestnut-vendor.

Here is a fellow who comes out of quod, and calls other people thieves.

Alphonse

(*a twelve-year-old, comes out of the wine-shop and says to* Crainquebille *in a tone of the sweetest politeness:*)

I say, guv'nor, is it true that it's quite comfortable in jail?

Crainquebille.

Dirty young cub! (*He gives him a kick.* Alphonse *goes in whimpering.*) It is your father who ought to be in jail, instead of growing rich by selling poison.

The Wineshop-keeper (*followed by his son*).
If it were not for your white hairs I would teach you to hit my son. (*To his son.*) Go in, you little varmint! [*They go in.*

Crainquebille (*to the* Chestnut-vendor)
Well, would you believe it?

The Chestnut-vendor.
What can you expect? He is right: you oughtn't to hit other folks' children, nor reproach them for having a father they never chose. My poor Crainquebille, for the last two months, since you came out, you are not the same man; you are hard to live with, and everything seems to taste sour to you. That wouldn't matter, but all you are good for nowadays is to raise your elbow.

Crainquebille.
I have never been a waster, but now and again I must have a glass for refreshment's sake and to put me on my legs. My inside burns me. And nothing picks you up like a drink.

The Chestnut-vendor.
That wouldn't matter so much either, but you are flabby and work-shy. A man in that condition is a man who is down and can't get up again. Everyone who passes tramples on him.

Crainquebille.

True enough. I haven't the courage I used to have. I am done for. The pitcher goes so often to the well that at last it breaks. And then, since that affair of mine in Court I have lost my character. I am no longer the same man. What can you expect? They took me up for shouting " bloody copper." It wasn't true. There was a doctor there with a ribbon in his coat who told them it wasn't true. They wouldn't hear anything. I allow you, the magistrates are very civil; they don't swear at one, but one can't explain things to them. They gave me two quid, and they hid my barrow away so that it took me a fortnight before I could lay my hands on it. And the whole thing is most extraordinary. On my soul, it is as if I had been acting in a play.

The Chestnut-vendor.

They gave you two quid? That is something new. They used not to do that.

Crainquebille.

To be just, they gave me two quid in the hand. And then a prison is quite decent. One cannot deny it. It is well kept and clean. You could eat off the floor. But when you come out there is no work, no way of earning a halfpenny. Everyone turns his back on you.

The Chestnut-vendor.
I will tell you what : change your neighbourhood.

Crainquebille.
Madame Bayard, at the boot-shop, she makes a face when I pass. She insults me, and it was her fault I was taken up. The beauty of it is, she still owes me that sevenpence. I should have claimed it just now, but she had a customer. Let her wait a little. She shall lose nothing by waiting.

The Chestnut-vendor.
Where are you going ?

Crainquebille.
I am going to talk to Madame Bayard.

The Chestnut-vendor.
You keep quiet.

Crainquebille.
Why, I have the right to claim my sevenpence. I want it; perhaps you will give it me ? If you will, say so.

The Chestnut-vendor.
Not to be done ; my old woman would tear my eyes out. I have given you enough—a shilling here, and two shillings there—these last two months.

CRAINQUEBILLE.
Am I to die like a dog ? I haven't got a farthing left.

THE CHESTNUT-VENDOR (*calling him back*).
Crainquebille . . . do you know what you ought to do ?

CRAINQUEBILLE.
What ?

THE CHESTNUT-VENDOR.
You ought to change your neighbourhood.

CRAINQUEBILLE.
That is impossible. I am like a goat that browses where she is tied up. She must browse even though there are only stones.

[MADAME BAYARD *is seeing her customer out; when the latter has turned the corner of the street,* MADAME BAYARD *comes straight to* CRAINQUEBILLE *and addresses him loudly.*

MADAME BAYARD.
What do you want with me ?

CRAINQUEBILLE.
It is no good glaring at me like that. I want my sevenpence.

MADAME BAYARD
(*coming down from her altitude*).
Your sevenpence?

CRAINQUEBILLE.
Yes, my sevenpence.

MADAME BAYARD.
To begin with, I forbid you to enter my shop as you did a moment ago. It is no way to behave.

CRAINQUEBILLE.
Maybe—but my sevenpence . . .

MADAME BAYARD.
I don't know what you mean. Moreover, understand this, one can owe nothing to people who have been in prison.

CRAINQUEBILLE.
You baggage!

MADAME BAYARD.
Ruffian! Oh! if only my husband were still alive!

CRAINQUEBILLE.
If I had your husband here, you old croaker, I would give him a sound kick to teach him to rob people and insult them afterwards.

Madame Bayard.
Where are the police?
> [*She goes in and fastens the shop-door.*

Crainquebille.
Keep it then! Keep it, thief that you are!

The Chestnut-vendor.
Thief, thieves, the word is never out of your mouth! All the world's a thief, according to you. It is true and, on the other hand, it isn't true. I'll tell you. We all have to live, and you can't live without injuring others—it is impossible—so . . .

La Souris.
Good evening, everyone.

The Chestnut-vendor.
Good evening, La Souris.

La Souris.
Feeling better, old Crainquebille? You don't remember me? La Souris. You know me well, all the same. You gave me a pear, tho' it was a bit over-ripe.

Crainquebille.
Possibly.

La Souris.

I am going to take a rest. I am living here. I am tired. Love us! when one has sweated all day long! I have been calling *La Patrie, La Presse, Le Soir,* till my throat is sore. When I have had a bite I shall get under the bed-clothes. Good night all.

The Chestnut-vendor.

You have no bed-clothes.

La Souris.

No bed-clothes? Come and look. I have made myself some out of newspapers and sacks.

Crainquebille.

You are in luck, old chap. It is two months since I slept on anything soft. (La Souris *goes indoors.*) And that's true. They turned me out of my attic. For thirty nights I have been sleeping in a stable on my barrow. It has never stopped raining, and the stable is flooded. To avoid drowning one must sit up and crouch over the stinking water, with the cats, and rats, and great spiders as big as pumpkins. And then, last night, the drain-pipe burst, the carts were all swimming in the sewage, bah! Why, they even put a guard at the door to prevent people from entering because the walls are shaky. They are like me, the walls, they won't stand up much longer. (*Seeing* MADAME LAURE *enter the wine-shop.*) Hallo! there is Madame Laure.

THE CHESTNUT-VENDOR.

Madame Laure is a steady woman, and doing well; and considering what she is, she knows her position. She does not drink at the bar. I bet you she will come out with a quart of something to drink at home with her friends.

CRAINQUEBILLE.

Madame Laure! I know her as if I were her Maker. She is a customer. A fine lady, sure enough.

THE CHESTNUT-VENDOR.

And a fine woman. (MADAME LAURE *comes out of the wine-shop.*) There, what did I tell you?

CRAINQUEBILLE.

Good day, Madame Laure.

MADAME LAURE (*to* THE CHESTNUT-VENDOR).

Two penn'orth of chestnuts. And mind they are hot.

CRAINQUEBILLE.

You do not remember me, Madame Laure? The costermonger.

Madame Laure.

Yes, I know. (*To* The Chestnut-vendor.) Don't give me those out of your bag. There's no knowing how long they have been cooling there.

The Chestnut-vendor.

They are piping hot; they are burning my fingers.

Crainquebille.

You don't remember me so easily because I have not got my barrow. People look at things differently sometimes. . . . And are you getting on all right, Madame Laure? (*He touches her on the arm.*) I am asking you—are you getting on all right?

Madame Laure.

Now then, Auverpin, hurry up with those chestnuts. I have people waiting for me. I have a party to-day. Only people whom I know.

Crainquebille.

Don't take your custom away from me, Madame Laure. You always did look at both sides of a sixpence, but you are a good customer, all the same.

Madame Laure (*to* The Chestnut-vendor).

Do them up quick. It is not pleasant to have a man talking to you who has been in trouble.

CRAINQUEBILLE.
What did you say?

MADAME LAURE.
I was not talking to you.

CRAINQUEBILLE.
You said I had been in trouble. Well, what about you? You have seen the inside of a Black Maria. If I had as many dollar pieces as you have been times in the police-van . . .

THE CHESTNUT-VENDOR.
There you go, cursing at my customers now. Shut up, or I'll put it across you.

MADAME LAURE.
Go along with you, you old Ticket-of-leave.

CRAINQUEBILLE.
You know all about it, you do. . . .
[*The apparition of a policeman, silent and watchful, ends the dispute.* MADAME LAURE *goes off majestically.*

LA SOURIS (*at the window*).
Shut your mouths. One can't sleep!

CRAINQUEBILLE.
B—h that she is . . . there is no greater b—h than that woman.

THE CHESTNUT-VENDOR (*packing up his stove*).
To go for a customer just as she is being served! You must have lost all sense of things. Clear out of my way. You may think yourself lucky that I did not give you in charge. (*Going off.*) A man to whom I have lent shillings and shillings a week for the last two months. But he doesn't know what's what.   [*The barman puts up the shutters.*

SCENE II.

CRAINQUEBILLE.
Hi! there, Auverpin! Auverpin! Listen! He hooks off. He won't listen to anything. What I have against that old hag is that they are all like her, all of them. They pretend not to know me; Madame Cointreau, Madame Lessenne, Madame Bayard. All of them. So, because one has been put away for a fortnight one isn't even good enough to sell leeks. Is it fair? Is there any sense in letting a decent fellow die of hunger because he has had trouble with the 'tecs? If I can't sell my

vegetables I can do nothing but starve. Why, I might have stolen, or murdered, or had the plague, it would not have been worse. And the cold and hunger. I have had nothing to eat. It's down and out with you, old Crainquebille. You're done. At times I am sorry I ever came out. . . . (*There is a policeman standing still in the background.* CRAINQUEBILLE *sees him and says:*) What a fool I am! I know the trick. Why shouldn't I make use of it? (*He goes quietly up to the policeman and in a weak and hesitating voice says:*) You bloody copper! (*The constable looks at* CRAINQUEBILLE, *not without sadness, but keenly and contemptuously. An interval.* CRAINQUEBILLE, *astonished, stammers:*) You bloody copper! that's what I say.

THE POLICE-CONSTABLE.

Well, you ought not to say it. You—ought—not—to say it. At your age you should know better. Move on!

CRAINQUEBILLE.

Why don't you run me in?

THE POLICE-CONSTABLE (*shaking his head*).

If I had to take up every sot who said what he oughtn't to, I should have my work cut out. And what good would it be?

CRAINQUEBILLE
(*overcome, remains a long time silent and stupefied; then says very gently:*)
I did not mean you when I said " bloody copper." It was not meant for anyone in particular. It was just a . . . a . . . notion.

THE CONSTABLE (*with gentle austerity*).
If it was just a notion or anything else, you ought not to have said it. Because when a man does his duty, and has much to put up with, you ought not to insult him with foolish words. . . . I tell you again, move on.

SCENE III.

LA SOURIS (*out of the window*).
Old Crainquebille! Old Crainquebille! Old Crainquebille!

CRAINQUEBILLE.
Hallo, who is that up there? Is it a miracle? It don't seem possible . . .

LA SOURIS.
Old Crainquebille . . .

CRAINQUEBILLE.
Oh, it's you!

LA SOURIS.
Where are you off to, like that, with no umbrella?

CRAINQUEBILLE.
Where am I off to?

LA SOURIS.
Yes.

CRAINQUEBILLE.
I am going to throw myself in the Seine.

LA SOURIS.
Don't do that. It is too cold and too wet.

CRAINQUEBILLE.
What do you want me to do?

LA SOURIS.
You must get a move on—you must do something for your living.

CRAINQUEBILLE.
Why?

LA SOURIS.
I dunno, but one must pull oneself out of it, somehow. You are up against it, but it won't last for ever. You'll sell your cabbages and carrots again soon, *I* tell you. Come up here. I've a loaf and some sausage, and a bottle. We'll have supper like a pair of toffs, and I'll make you a bed like

mine, with sacks and papers, and we'll see if things aren't better to-morrow. So come on up, my ancient.

CRAINQUEBILLE.

You are young—you still have some good in you. It's a bad world, but you are no part of it, yet. Kid though you are, you can say that you have been the saving of a man. No great matter, perhaps. Nothing to boast of—it won't stop the moon going round, it won't make the state any handsomer—but you have saved a man.

[CRAINQUEBILLE, *with bowed head and arms drooped by his sides, goes up without more words.*

[In this translation of *Crainquebille* in its dramatic form, an attempt has been made to provide an English stage version. Consequently, it has been freely adapted in places.—ED.]

THE COMEDY OF A MAN WHO MARRIED A DUMB WIFE

A room on the ground floor in the house of M. LÉONARD BOTAL. *On the left the door gives on the Rue Dauphine in Paris; when the door opens the Pont Neuf is visible. On the right a door opens into the kitchen; at the back a wooden staircase leads to the upper rooms. Against the walls hang portraits of magistrates in their robes, and immense cupboards are ranged, crammed and overflowing with bags, books, papers, and parchments. A pair of steps on wheels gives access to the top of the cupboards. A writing-table, chairs, and stuffed arm-chairs, and a spinning-wheel.*

THE COMEDY OF A MAN WHO MARRIED A DUMB WIFE

ACT I.

Scene I.

GILLES BOISCOURTIER, ALIZON, *then* MAÎTRE ADAM FUMÉE, *and* M. LÉONARD BOTAL.

[GILLES BOISCOURTIER *is scribbling and yawning when* ALIZON *the servant enters with a large basket on each arm. As soon as he sees her,* GILLES BOISCOURTIER *pounces on her.*

ALIZON.

Holy Virgin! How long has it been the fashion to swoop on a body like a wild thing, in a room open to all comers, too?

GILLES

(*drawing a bottle of wine from one of the baskets*).

Don't squawk, you little goose. No one is going to pluck you. You're not worth it.

ALIZON.

Will you be so good as to leave the Judge's wine alone, you thief!

[*She puts her baskets on the ground, snatches the bottle back, boxes the secretary's ears, picks up her baskets again, and flies to the kitchen, of which the fireplace can be seen through the half-open door.*

MAÎTRE ADAM FUMÉE *enters.*

ADAM.

Isn't this the house of M. Léonard Botal, Judge of the civil and criminal courts?

GILLES.

It is, monsieur, and at this moment you are speaking to his secretary, Gilles Boiscourtier, at your service.

ADAM.

Well, my lad, go and tell him that his old fellow-student, Maître Adam Fumée, advocate, is come to discuss some business.

[*From outside comes the voice of a hawker calling:* "*Chickweed for your cage-birds.*"

GILLES.

Monsieur, here he is himself.

[LÉONARD BOTAL *comes down the staircase.* GILLES *retires into the kitchen.*

Adam.

Welcome, M. Léonard Botal, I am delighted to see you once again.

Léonard.

Good day, Maître Adam Fumée, and how have you been all the long time since I last had the pleasure of seeing you?

Adam.

Very well; and I hope you can say the same, sir?

Léonard.

What good wind blows you here, Maître Adam Fumée?

Adam.

I come from Chartres on purpose to lodge a memorial in favour of a young lady, an orphan, whose . . .

Léonard.

Do you remember the days, Maître Adam Fumée, when we studied law at the University of Orleans?

Adam.

Yes—we used to play the flute, sup with the ladies, and dance from morning till night. . . . I am come, my dear sir and comrade, to lodge a memorial in favour of a young lady, an orphan, whose case is pending in your court.

LÉONARD.
Can she pay?

ADAM.
She is a young orphan. . . .

LÉONARD.
I quite understand, but can she pay?

ADAM.
She is a young orphan who has been plundered by her guardian, who has left her nothing but her eyes to cry with. If she wins her case she will be rich again, and will bestow substantial tokens of her gratitude.

LÉONARD.
(*taking the paper that* MAÎTRE ADAM *holds out*).
We will look into the matter.

ADAM.
Thank you, my dear sir and comrade.

LÉONARD.
We will investigate her case without fear or favour.

ADAM.
There is no need to tell me so. But—come now—are things going as well with you as you could wish? You seem careworn. And yet you have dropped in for a good thing.

LÉONARD.
I paid a good price for it, and I was not taken in.

ADAM.
Perhaps you are weary of living alone ? Have you no thought of marrying ?

LÉONARD.
What ? you do not know, Maître Adam, that I am newly wed ? I married last month, a young lady from the provinces, of good family and appearance—Catherine Momichel, the seventh daughter of the Judge of the Criminal Court at Salency. Unhappily, she is dumb, and that is my trouble.

ADAM.
Your wife dumb ?

LÉONARD.
Alas !

ADAM.
Quite dumb ?

LÉONARD.
Dumb as a fish.

ADAM.
Did you not notice it before you married her ?

LÉONARD.

It would have been scarcely possible not to remark it. But it did not affect me as it does to-day. I reflected that she was good-looking, and had means, and I only thought of the blessings she was bringing me and of the pleasure I should have in her. But now these considerations appeal to me less, and I heartily wish that she could speak. It would be gratifying to my mental faculties and advantageous for my household. The residence of a judge needs—what? A woman of charm, who receives litigants pleasantly, and leads them gently by tactful observations to proffer gifts in order that their cases may receive closer attention. People only give when they are encouraged to give. A wife with a well-turned phrase and a timely gesture will extract a ham from this one, a piece of cloth from that—from a third wine or poultry. But this poor dumb thing of a Catherine never gets anything. Whereas the kitchen, the cellar, the stable, and barns of my learned brothers are bursting with good things, thanks to their wives, I get hardly enough to keep the pot boiling. So you may see, Maître Adam Fumée, what harm it does me to have a dumb wife. I am worth the half of what I should be . . . and the worst of it is that it is making me melancholy and distraught.

ADAM.

There is no cause, sir. On close consideration

your lot would disclose advantages which are not to be despised.

Léonard.

You don't know what it is like, Maître Adam. When I take my wife in my arms—and she is as shapely as the finest of statues, at least, so she seems to me, and, i'faith, she has no more to say for herself—I am oddly troubled and feel curiously ill at ease. I even ask myself if I have not to do with an image, an automaton, a magic doll, some contrivance due to the sorcerer's arts, rather than with one of God's creatures; and sometimes, of a morning, I am tempted to leap out of my bed to escape from spells.

Adam.

What strange fancies!

Léonard.

And that is not all. Living with the dumb, I am becoming dumb myself. From time to time I catch myself expressing myself in signs, as she does. The other day, on the bench, I actually passed sentence in dumb-show, and condemned a man to the galleys simply by gesture and pantomime.

Adam.

There is no need to say more. One can understand that a dumb wife is poor at response. And one does not care about talking when one never gets a reply.

Léonard.
Now you know the reason of my depression.

Adam.
I have no wish to vex you, and I think you have just and sufficient cause. But there may be a way to put a stop to this. Tell me: is your wife deaf as well as dumb?

Léonard.
Catherine is no more deaf than you or I. Even less, if I may say so. She can hear the grass growing.

Adam.
If that is the case, you may take hope. When doctors, apothecaries, and surgeons succeed in giving speech to a deaf-mute the utterance is as lifeless as his own hearing. He hears neither what is said to him nor what he says himself. It is otherwise with mutes who can hear. It is a mere trifle for the doctor to loosen the tongue of such a one. The operation is so slight that it is daily performed on puppies who are backward in barking. Does it require a countryman such as I am to inform you that a famous doctor, who lives but a few steps from your dwelling in the Carrefour Buci, at the sign of the Dragon, Master Simon Colline, is

renowned for loosing the tongues of the ladies of Paris. With a turn of the wrist he will set flowing from the mouth of your good lady a flood of well-articulated words, even as on turning a tap the imprisoned water flows forth with a gentle gurgle.

Léonard.

Is this true, Maître Adam ? You are not deceiving me ? You are not speaking for a client ?

Adam.

I speak as your friend, and tell you the simple truth.

Léonard.

Then I will send for this celebrated doctor; and that without an instant's delay.

Adam.

As you like. But before calling him in, reflect soberly on what is the wisest course. For, all things considered, if a dumb wife has her drawbacks, she also has her advantages. Good evening, my dear sir and comrade. Believe me your friend, and read my memorial, I beg of you. If you exercise your justice in favour of a young orphan plundered by her greedy guardian, you shall have no cause to repent.

LÉONARD.
Return ere long, Maître Adam. I shall have prepared my judgment.   [MAÎTRE ADAM *leaves.*

SCENE II.

LÉONARD, *then* GILLES, *then* CATHERINE.

LÉONARD (*calling*).
Gilles! Gilles! He does not hear me, the young rip! He is in the kitchen as usual, upsetting the pots and the maids. Glutton and rake that he is! Gilles! Gilles! you scamp! you rascal!

GILLES.
Here I am, your worship.

LÉONARD.
Well, young man, go as fast as you can to the famous doctor who lives in the Carrefour Buci, at the sign of the Dragon—Master Simon Colline—and tell him to come at once to this house to treat a dumb woman.

GILLES.
Yes, sir.

LÉONARD.

Go straight there, mind, and don't linger on the Pont Neuf watching the boatmen. I know you, you vagabond. You haven't your equal when it comes to cheating.

GILLES.

You judge me wrongly, sir——

LÉONARD.

Off with you—and bring the famous doctor.

GILLES.

Yes, sir. [*He goes.*

LÉONARD

(*seated before his table, covered with legal documents*).

I have fourteen judgments to deliver to-day, without counting the decree relating to the ward of Maître Adam Fumée. And it's hard work, for a judgment does no credit to the judge unless it be well turned, subtle, elegant, and adorned with every ornament of style and thought. It must sparkle with ideas, and juggle with words. Where should one embody wit if not in a judgment?

[CATHERINE, *who has come down the staircase, takes her place at the spinning-wheel, near the table. She smiles at her husband and prepares to spin.*

LÉONARD (*stops writing*).

Good morning, my love. I did not even hear you. You are like one of those creatures of fable who seem to float in the air, or like a dream sent by the gods to happy mortals, as the poets tell.

[*A countryman is heard passing in the street, crying:* "*Fine watercress, good for the blood, three-farthings a bundle.*"

LÉONARD.

My love, you are one of Nature's marvels, a person accomplished in every way: only speech is lacking in you. Would you not be very pleased to acquire it? Would you not be happy if all the pretty thoughts one guesses from your eyes could pass your lips? Would it not be a satisfaction to you to exhibit your wit? Would it not please you to tell your husband that you love him? Would it not seem sweet to you to call him your treasure and sweetheart? No doubt it would . . . (*A street-hawker is heard crying as he passes:* "*Dips— cotton dips! Burn brighter than any star!*") Well, I have good news for you, my love. A clever doctor will be here presently who will make you speak. (CATHERINE *gives signs of satisfaction.*) He will loose your tongue without hurting you.

[CATHERINE *displays her joy by graceful gesturing and posturing. A blind man is heard passing along the street, singing a bourrée to the bagpipes:*

>Fish, gaily sporting,
>One comes to catch you,
>Tra-la-lal-la.
>Youth, idly courting,
>Mill-maiden frail !
>Schemes to attach you
>Past all avail.

[*The blind man in a lugubrious voice:* "Charity, for the love of God, good ladies and gentlemen." *He appears on the doorstep and continues to sing:*

>Riverward wend you,
>Arm clipped in arm,
>Tra-la-lal-la.
>Mill-maiden, send you
>Take no alarm !
>Trip you and bend you,
>Flaunting each charm,
>Tra-la-lal-la.

[CATHERINE *starts dancing the bourrée with the blind man; he takes up his song again:*

>Mill-maiden, send you
>Come not to harm !
>Tra-la-lal-la.

[*The blind man stops his playing and dancing to drone out in a formidable and cavernous voice:* "*Charity, for the love of God, good ladies and gentlemen.*"]

Léonard
(*who, immersed in his papers, has seen nothing, chases him out, calling him*)

Rogue, money-grubber, vagabond! (*Throwing brief-bags at his head.—To* Catherine, *who has gone back to her spinning-wheel.*) My love, since you came down I have not wasted my time. I have sent fourteen men and six women to the stocks; distributed between seventeen individuals... (*he reckons up.*) ... Six, twenty-four ... thirty-two ... forty-four ... forty-seven and nine ... fifty-six, and eleven, sixty-seven, and ten, seventy-seven, and eight, eighty-five, and twenty, one hundred and five. A hundred and five years at the galleys. Does that not give you a high notion of a judge's powers, and can I help feeling a little proud? (Catherine, *who has stopped spinning, leans against the table and looks smilingly at her husband. Then she seats herself on the table all covered with bags full of legal documents.* Léonard, *pretending to pull the bags from under her.*) My love, you are hiding some arch criminals from justice. Thieves and murderers. . . . I will not pursue them, however . . . their place of refuge is sacred.

[*A sweep is heard crying without:* "Sweep

your chimneys, young ladies, from top to bottom." Léonard *and* Catherine *embrace across the table. But seeing the Faculty coming,* Catherine *escapes up the stairs.*

Scene III.

Léonard, Gilles, Master Simon Colline, Master Séraphin Dulaurier, *then* Master Jean Maugier, *then* Alizon.

Gilles.
Your worship, here is the great doctor you have summoned.

Master Simon.
Yes, I am Master Simon Colline, in person. And here is Master Jean Maugier, the surgeon. You have asked for our attendance?

Léonard.
Yes, sir, to give a dumb woman speech.

Simon.
It is well. We wait the arrival of Master Seraphin Dulaurier, the apothecary. As soon as he comes we will operate according to our knowledge and understanding.

LÉONARD.

Ah, does it need an apothecary, then, to make the dumb speak?

SIMON.

Yes, sir, and whoever doubts it totally ignores the inter-relation of organs and their mutual dependence. Master Séraphin Dulaurier will not be long in coming.

JEAN MAUGIER
(*suddenly bawling with the voice of a Stentor*).

Oh! how grateful we should be to learned doctors such as Master Simon Colline, who labour to keep us in health, and tend us in sickness. Oh! how worthy of all praise and blessing are these good doctors who practise their profession in accordance with the laws of instructed knowledge and long experience.

SIMON (*bowing slightly*).
You are too kind, Master Jean Maugier.

LÉONARD.

Will you take some refreshment, gentlemen, while we are waiting for the good apothecary?

SIMON.

Willingly.

JEAN.

With pleasure.

Léonard.
So, Master Simon Colline, you can perform a little operation which will enable my wife to speak?

Simon.
I will order the operation, that is to say. I give the orders, Master Jean Maugier executes them . . . Have you your instruments, Master Jean?

Jean.
Yes, Master. . . . (*He exhibits a saw three feet long with two-inch teeth, knives, pincers, shears, a centre-bit, a gigantic auger, a probe, etc.*)

Enter ALIZON, *with wine.*

Léonard.
I trust, gentlemen, that you are not going to make use of all those?

Simon.
It doesn't answer to be short of an instrument when operating.

Léonard.
Drink, gentlemen.

Simon.
This light wine is not bad.

Léonard.
You are too good. It is of my own growing.

SIMON.
You may send me a hogshead of it.

LÉONARD
(*to* GILLES, *who pours himself a bumper*).
I didn't ask you to drink, you scamp.

JEAN
(*looking out of the window into the street*).
Here is Master Séraphin Dulaurier, the apothecary.

MASTER SÉRAPHIN *enters*.

SIMON.
And here is his mule ... no, it is Master Séraphin himself. One never knows which. Drink, Master Séraphin. It is only just drawn.

SÉRAPHIN.
Your health, my masters!

SIMON (*to* ALIZON).
Pour, my beauty. Pour right and left, pour here and there. Whatever way she turns she shows abundant charms. Are you not uplifted, my child, by your comeliness?

ALIZON.
There is not much reason to be proud for all the

profit I get by it. Charms bring in little enough unless they are decked out in silk and satin.

SÉRAPHIN.
Your health, my masters!

ALIZON.
They like to have their jest with one. But not if it costs them anything.
[*They all drink, and make* ALIZON *do so.*

SIMON.
Now we are all ready we may as well go up to see the patient.

LÉONARD.
I will show you the way, gentlemen.
[*He goes up the stairs.*

SIMON.
After you, Master Maugier, after you.

JEAN (*glass in hand*).
I yield to you, for it's well known that the place of honour is at the rear.

SIMON.
After you, Master Séraphin.
[MASTER SÉRAPHIN *follows* LÉONARD, *carrying a bottle.*

SIMON

(*having stuck a bottle in each pocket of his gown and kissed the serving-maid, climbs the stairs, singing*).

A bowl! A bowl! A bowl!
What never a parting bowl?
Good friends were verily dull of soul
To part with never a bowl!

[ALIZON, *having given* GILLES *a box on the ears for trying to kiss her, climbs up last. They can still be heard, all singing in chorus:* "*A bowl! A bowl! A bowl!*" *etc.*

ACT II.

SCENE I.

LÉONARD, MAÎTRE ADAM.

ADAM.
Good evening, worshipful sir, how do I find you?

LÉONARD.
Well enough—and you?

Adam.

Never better. Forgive my importunity, dear sir and comrade. Have you looked into this affair of my young ward plundered by her guardian?

Léonard.

Not yet, Maître Adam. But what's that you say? You have plundered your ward?

Adam.

Do not imagine such a thing! I say " my ward " from pure friendship. I am not her guardian, thank God! I am her counsel. And if she recover her property, which is large, I shall marry her. I have already taken the precaution to inspire her with love for me. That is why I shall be grateful if you will look into her case as promptly as possible. You have only to read my memorial. It contains everything that is pertinent.

Léonard.

Your memorial, Maître Adam, is there on my table. I should have acquainted myself with it ere now had I not been busy. I have had the élite of the medical Faculty here, and it was on your advice that I had all this to-do.

Adam.

What do you mean?

Léonard.

I called in the celebrated doctor you spoke of—Master Simon Colline; he came with a surgeon and an apothecary; he examined my wife from head to foot to see if she was dumb. Then the surgeon cut the string of my dear Catherine's tongue, the apothecary gave her a dose, and she spoke.

Adam.

She spoke! Was a dose necessary for that?

Léonard.

Yes—by reason of the sympathy of the organs.

Adam.

Ah! . . . At any rate, the essential thing is that she has spoken. What did she say?

Léonard.

She said: "Bring me the mirror." And then, seeing me much moved, she said: "My ownest, you must give me a satin gown and a hood with a velvet binding for my birthday."

Adam.

And she continues to speak?

Léonard.

She hasn't stopped since.

Adam.

And you don't thank me for the advice I gave you ? You don't thank me for making this great doctor known to you ? Are you not well pleased to hear your wife speak ?

Léonard.

Yes, yes. I thank you with all my heart, Maître Adam Fumée, and it is with pleasure that I hear my wife speak.

Adam.

No, you don't show as much satisfaction as you should. There is something that vexes you and that you don't tell me.

Léonard.

Whence do you get that notion ?

Adam.

From your face. What is it that annoys you ? Does not your good lady speak well ?

Léonard.

She speaks well and speaks much. I confess to you that the abundance of her speech would inconvenience me if she kept it up at the force of the first rush.

Adam.

I foresaw it to some extent. But one must not despair about it all at once. The flow of words will diminish, perhaps. It is the first bubbling over of a spring opened over-suddenly. . . . My congratulations to you, worshipful sir. My ward's name is Ermeline de la Garandière. Do not forget her name. Deal favourably with her and you shall not have ingratitude to face. I will come back this evening.

Léonard.

Maître Adam Fumée, I will go and consider your case at once. [Maître Adam Fumée *leaves*.

Scene II.

Léonard, *then* Catherine.

Léonard (*reading*).

Memorial on behalf of Ermeline - Jacinthe - Marthe de la Garandière.

Catherine
(*who has set herself down by her spinning-wheel, beside the table—with volubility*).

What are you at, my friend ? You seem engrossed. You do a great deal of work. Are you not afraid of some ill result? One should rest at times. But you don't tell me what you are busied with, my friend?

LÉONARD.

My love! ...

CATHERINE.

Is it such a great secret, then? Mustn't I know it? ...

LÉONARD.

My love, I ...

CATHERINE.

If it's a secret, don't tell me.

LÉONARD.

Give me time to reply. I am getting up a case, and preparing my judgment on it.

CATHERINE.

Passing judgment is an important matter.

LÉONARD.

No doubt of that. Not only does the honour, the liberty, and sometimes the life of people depend on it, but beyond that the judge must show the profundity of his intelligence and the polish of his language.

CATHERINE.

Get along with your case, then, and prepare your judgment, my friend. I will say nothing.

Léonard.
Good. . . . The demoiselle Ermeline-Jacinthe-Marthe de la Garandière . . .

Catherine.
Which do you think would suit me best, a damask gown or simply a coat all velvet—cut Turkish fashion ?

Léonard.
I don't know, I . . .

Catherine.
It seems to me that a flowered satin would be most suitable to my age, more especially if it were light-coloured and the flowers small . . .

Léonard.
I dare say, but . . .

Catherine.
And don't you think, my friend, that it would be unbecoming to exaggerate the fullness of the hoops ? Of course, a skirt should stand out; without that one would not look dressed—one must not skimp the skirt. But you don't want me to be able to hide two gallants under my hoops, do you, my friend ? The fashion will not last. One of these days ladies of quality will abandon it, and

the middle-class will follow their example. Do you not think so?

Léonard.

I agree, but . . .

Catherine.

And then one must pay heed to the style of shoe. A woman is judged by her foot, and you can tell a really elegant woman by her shoes. You think so, too, do you not?

Léonard.

Yes, but . . .

Catherine.

Go on with your judgment—I will say no more.

Léonard.

That's right. (*Reading and taking notes.*) Whereas the guardian of the said demoiselle, Hugues Thomassin, lord of the manor of Piédeloup, has robbed the said demoiselle of her . . .

Catherine.

My dear, if one may believe the wife of the president of Montbadon, society is very corrupt; it is on the road to ruin; young people of to-day prefer to traffic with rich old ladies rather than make an honest marriage; and meanwhile well-conducted girls waste their sweetness. Can such things be? Tell me, my dear.

LÉONARD.

My dear, either keep silent a moment, or be good enough to carry your conversation elsewhere. I don't know where I am.

CATHERINE.

Don't be put out, my dear. I will not say another word.

LÉONARD.

Thank goodness. . . . (*Writing.*) The said Seigneur de Piédeloup, both by peculations at haytime and the cider season . . .

CATHERINE.

My dear, for to-night's supper we have minced mutton and the remains of a goose, the gift of a client. Tell me if it is enough? Will it satisfy you? I detest meanness and like an abundant table; but what is the use of dishing up good things that are carried untouched back to the kitchen? Living is become so expensive. At the poulterer's, the greengrocer's, the butcher's, the fruiterer's, everything has gone up so in price that soon we shall do better to order our meals in from outside.

LÉONARD.

I beg of you . . . (*Writing.*) Orphan from her birth . . .

CATHERINE.

That's what we shall come to, you will see. For a chicken, a partridge, a hare, cost less roasted and larded than bought fresh killed at the market. And that because the cook-shop people who buy on a large scale get them cheap, and that enables them to sell again at a moderate price. I don't say that we should order in our meals every day from the restaurant. Simple cooking at home is nicer; but when one wants to entertain friends, to give a dinner, it is easier done and less expensive to order it in. The restaurant people and the confectioners will, in less than an hour, send you round a dinner for a dozen, for twenty, for fifty people; from the restaurant you get your meat and poultry, and a man to superintend them, your jellies, sauces, and stews; from the confectioner your pies and tarts, entrées, and dessert. It is most convenient. You agree with me, Léonard?

LÉONARD.

For pity's sake . . . !

CATHERINE.

It is not surprising that everything gets dearer. The luxury of the table becomes daily more pronounced. Let a relative or a friend dine with you and it is no longer a matter of three courses, roast, boiled, and sweet. One must have meat dishes done in five or six different ways, with so many sauces, and minces, and kinds of pastry that it is a perfect *omnium gatherum*. Don't you find it excessive, my dear? I, for one, cannot understand the pleasure they find in stuffing themselves with so much food. Not that I disdain good things, I enjoy them. I like a little, but that good. I am particularly fond of cocks' combs and the chokes of artichokes. And you, Léonard, haven't you a weakness for tripe and chitterlings? Fie! how can anyone like such things?

LÉONARD (*clutching his head with his hands*).
I shall go mad. I feel that I shall go mad.

CATHERINE.
My dear, I won't say another word, for by speaking I may distract you from your work.

LÉONARD.
If you would only do what you say.

CATHERINE.
I won't open my mouth.

LÉONARD.
Wonderful!

CATHERINE.
You see—I am not saying a word.

LÉONARD.

Yes.

CATHERINE.

I will let you work in quiet.

LÉONARD.

Yes.

CATHERINE.

And formulate your judgment in peace. Will it soon be done?

LÉONARD.

Never, unless you hold your tongue. (*Writing.*) Item. A hundred and twenty livres of income which this unworthy guardian has embezzled from this poor orphan . . .

CATHERINE.

Listen! Hush! Listen! Is not someone calling "Fire"? I thought I heard it. But perhaps I was mistaken. Is there anything more alarming than a fire? It is even more terrible than water. Last year I saw the burning of the houses on the Pont-au-Change. The turmoil! The havoc! The inhabitants threw their furniture into the river. Threw themselves out of the windows. They did not know what they were doing. Fear had deprived them of their senses.

LÉONARD.
Lord have mercy on me!

CATHERINE.
Why do you groan, my friend? Tell me what troubles you?

LÉONARD.
I can bear no more.

CATHERINE.
Rest, Léonard—you must not tire yourself so. It is not reasonable, and it would be wrong of you to . . .

LÉONARD.
Will you never hold your tongue?

CATHERINE.
Don't get angry, my friend. I won't say another word.

LÉONARD.
Heaven grant it!

CATHERINE (*looking out of the window*).
Ah! there is Madame de la Bruine coming, the Procureur's wife; she is wearing a hood bound with silk and a great puce-coloured mantle over a brocade dress. She is followed by a lackey as withered as a smoked herring. Léonard, she is looking this way:

she looks as if she were coming to call. Make haste and put the chairs forward ready for her—people must be received according to their rank and station. She is just stopping at the door. No, she is passing. She is gone on. Perhaps I was mistaken. Perhaps it was not she. One isn't always sure of people. But if it was not she, it was someone very like her, someone very like her, indeed. Now I think of it I am sure that it was she, there could not be a woman in Paris so like Madame de la Bruine. My dear, my dear—wouldn't you have been glad if Madame de la Bruine had called on us? (*She sits on the table.*) You who don't like talkative women, it is well for you that you didn't marry her. She chatters like a magpie, she does nothing but gabble from morning till night. What a jabberer! And she retails stories sometimes that are very little to her credit.

[LEONARD, *beside himself, mounts the step-ladder with his writing materials, and sits on one of the steps, where he tries to write.*

CATHERINE.

She will start enumerating all the presents her husband receives. The account is precise. (*She ascends the other side of the steps and sits down facing LEONARD.*) Now does it interest us that the Monsieur de la Bruine gets game, flour, fish, or loaves of sugar sent him? But Madame de la

Bruine takes good care not to tell that one day her husband received a big pie from Amiens, and that when he opened it he only found a big pair of horns.

LÉONARD.

My head will burst!

[*He takes refuge on the top of the cupboard with his papers and writing materials.*

CATHERINE (*at the very top of the ladder*).

Did you see the procuress? for, after all, since she is the wife of a procureur she must be a procuress. She wears an embroidered hood like a princess. Don't you think it absurd? but nowadays everybody must be above his station, men and women alike. Young lawyers' clerks want to pass for gentlemen; they wear gold chains and clasps and plumed hats. . . . In spite of that one can easily see what they are.

LÉONARD (*on the cupboard*).

I have got to that pitch that I am no longer answerable for myself, and I feel capable of any crime. (*Calls.*) Gilles! Gilles! Gilles! you scoundrel! Gilles! Alizon! Gilles! Gilles! (*Enter* GILLES.) Go quickly and find the celebrated doctor in the Carrefour Buci, Master Simon Colline, and tell him to come back at once to a case of quite another kind from the former one, but just as pressing.

GILLES.
Yes, your worship. [He goes.

CATHERINE.
What is the matter, my friend? You seem heated. Perhaps because the weather is oppressive. ... No? It is the east wind, don't you think? or the fish you had for dinner?

LÉONARD
(*exhibiting signs of frenzy on his cupboard-top*).
Non omnia possumus omnes. The Swiss are toss-pots, the draper measures ribbon, monks beg, little birds mess everywhere, and women cackle like all possessed! Oh! how I repent, you jade, that I had your tongue loosed! But wait a little. The great doctor will shortly make you more dumb than you were before.

[*He picks up armfuls of the bags of papers piled on the cupboard, where he has taken refuge, and throws them at* CATHERINE'S *head, who descends with agility from the ladder and flies in fright up the stairs, crying out:*

CATHERINE.
Help! Help! Murder! My husband's gone mad! Help!

LÉONARD.
Alizon! Alizon! [ALIZON *enters,*

ALIZON.

What a life! Monsieur, are you going to turn murderer?

LÉONARD.

Alizon, follow her—keep your eye on her—don't let her come down. As you value your life, Alizon, don't let her come down. If I listen to her any more I shall become mad, and God knows to what extremities I may be provoked against her and against you. Begone!

[ALIZON *goes up the stairs.*

SCENE III.

LÉONARD, MAÎTRE ADAM, MADEMOISELLE DE LE GARANDIÈRE, *followed by a lackey carrying a basket.*

ADAM.

Suffer me, worshipful sir, to touch your heart and move your bowels of compassion, by presenting to you the young orphaned lady who, plundered by a grasping guardian, implores your justice. Her eyes will speak to you better than my voice. Mademoiselle de la Garandière comes to you with prayers and tears; thereto she joins a ham, two game pies, a goose, and two ducklings. She dares to hope a favourable judgment in exchange.

LÉONARD.
Mademoiselle, you awaken my interest. Have you anything to add in support of your cause ?

MLLE DE LA G.
You are too good, sir. I abide by what my counsel has just said.

LÉONARD.
Is that all ?

MLLE DE LA G.
Yes, sir.

LÉONARD.
She speaks well—and briefly. This orphan moves me. (*To the footman.*) Take your bundle into the kitchen. (*The footman goes.—To* MAÎTRE ADAM.) Maître Adam, when you came in I was formulating the judgment I shall presently enter in the matter of this young lady.

[*He comes down from the cupboard.*

ADAM.
What ! on top of that cupboard ?

LÉONARD.
I don't know what's come over me. My head is very bad. Would you like to hear the judgment ? I want to read it over for my own sake. (*Reads.*) Whereas the demoiselle de le Garandière, orphan

from her birth, has fraudulently and by deceit conveyed away from the said Piédeloup her guardian ten crops of hay, twenty-four pounds of fish from private waters, and whereas there is nothing so terrifying as a fire, and whereas the Procureur has received a pie from Amiens in which was a pair of horns . . .

ADAM.

What, in Heaven's name, are you reading?

LÉONARD.

Do not ask me. I don't know myself. I feel as if some demon had been braying my brains in a mortar for two hours past. And it is your fault, Maître Adam Fumée. If the worthy doctor had not restored my wife's speech . . .

ADAM.

Do not blame me, Monsieur Léonard. I warned you. I told you plainly that you should think twice before you loosened a woman's tongue.

LÉONARD.

Ah, Maître Adam Fumée, how I regret the time when Catherine was dumb. No. Nature has no more terrible scourge than a talkative woman. . . . But I count on the doctors annulling their cruel gift. I have sent for them, and here is the surgeon even now.

Scene IV.

The same. Master Jean Maugier, *then* Master Simon Colline, *and* Master Séraphin Dulaurier, *followed by two little boys from the apothecary's.*

MAUGIER.

Worshipful sir, I have the honour to greet you. Here is Master Simon Colline approaching on his mule, followed by Master Séraphin Dulaurier, the apothecary. Round him surges an adoring crowd; serving-maids holding up their skirts, pastrycook's boys with baskets on their heads, form his escort. (*Enter* Master Simon Colline *and his following.*) Oh, how rightly is Master Simon Colline the cynosure of every eye when he passes through the city in gown and cap, hood and bands. Oh, how grateful we should be to these good doctors who labour to keep us in health and who tend us when . . .

SIMON (*to* Master Jean Maugier).
Enough! that will do.

LÉONARD.

Master Simon Colline, I was impatient to see you. I want your services at once.

SIMON.

For yourself, sir? What is your trouble? Where do you suffer?

LÉONARD.

No. For my wife—for her who was dumb.

SIMON.

Does she experience any inconvenience?

LÉONARD.

None. It is I who am inconvenienced.

SIMON.

How is this? It is you who are inconvenienced, and it is your wife you would have healed?

LÉONARD.

Master Simon Colline, she talks too much. She was to be made to speak, but not to this extent. Since you cured her dumbness she is driving me mad. I can endure her talk no longer. I have called you in to make her dumb once more.

SIMON.

It is impossible.

LÉONARD.

What do you say? You cannot take away the speech that you gave?

SIMON.
No. I cannot. My art is great, but it cannot do that.

MAUGIER.
It is an impossibility for us.

SÉRAPHIN.
All our ministrations can do nothing here.

SIMON.
We have remedies to make women speak—we have none to make them silent.

LÉONARD.
You have none ? What is this you tell me ? You drive me to despair.

SIMON.
Alas, worshipful sir, there is no elixir, balm, sovran recipe, opiate, unguent, plaster, local application, electuary, or panacea to heal intemperance of the glottis in woman. Theriac and orvietan are without virtue here, and all the herbs prescribed by Dioscorides would work nothing.

LÉONARD.
Do you speak truth ?

SIMON.
You insult me if you doubt it.

LÉONARD.
In that case I am a lost man. There is nothing left for me but to throw myself into the Seine with a stone round my neck. I cannot live in this uproar. If you do not want me to drown myself out of hand, you must find me a remedy, gentlemen.

SIMON.
There is none, as I have told you, for your wife. But there is one for you, if you consent to make use of it.

LÉONARD.
You restore me some hope. Explain yourself, I beg.

SIMON.
Against a woman's chatter there is one single remedy. It is the husband's deafness.

LÉONARD.
What do you mean?

SIMON.
I mean what I say.

ADAM.
Do you not understand? It is the finest in-

vention there is. Being unable to make your wife dumb, this great doctor offers to make you deaf.

LÉONARD.
Make me deaf once and for all ?

SIMON.
Without a doubt. I will heal you instantly and radically of your honoured wife's verbal incontinence, by cophosis.

LÉONARD.
Cophosis ? What is cophosis ?

SIMON.
It is what is vulgarly called deafness. Do you see any drawbacks to being deaf ?

LÉONARD.
Yes, I do. For, indeed, there are drawbacks.

MAUGIER.
Do you think so ?

SÉRAPHIN.
What are they ?

SIMON.
You are a judge. What drawback is there in a judge being deaf ?

ADAM.

None. You may believe me. I frequent the Courts. There is none.

SIMON.

Would justice come to any harm?

ADAM.

No harm would come of it. On the contrary, Monsieur Léonard Botal would hear neither advocates nor their clients, and would no longer run the risk of being taken in by falsehoods.

LÉONARD.

That is true.

ADAM.

He would be all the better judge.

LÉONARD.

Maybe . . .

ADAM.

You need have no doubt.

LÉONARD.

But how do you work this—this— —

MAUGIER.

Cure— —

SIMON.

Cophosis or deafness may be procured in several ways. It is produced by otorrhœa, by inflammation of the parotid, by sclerosis of the ear, by otitis, or by ankylosis of the small bones. But these various methods are long and painful.

LÉONARD.

I reject them. I reject them all emphatically.

SIMON.

You are wise. It is much better to induce cophosis by means of a certain white powder which I have in my pouch, a pinch of which introduced into the ear is enough to make you deaf as a post, or as unhearing as Heaven in an angry mood.

LÉONARD.

Thank you for nothing, Master Simon Colline; keep your powder. . . . I do not wish to be deaf.

SIMON.

What, you won't be deaf? You reject cophosis? You flee from the cure you but lately implored? It is all too common a spectacle and one well calculated to grieve the soul of a good doctor, to see a refractory patient reject salutary remedies . . .

MAUGIER.
... Avoid the ministrations which could comfort his sufferings. ...

SÉRAPHIN.
... And refuse to be healed.

ADAM.
Do not decide so hurriedly, Monsieur Léonard Botal, nor deliberately reject an evil which would shield you from a greater one.

LÉONARD.
No. I don't want to be deaf. I will have none of this powder.

SCENE V.

The same. ALIZON, *then* CATHERINE.

ALIZON (*rushing downstairs, holding her ears*).
I can stand it no more. My head is bursting. It is not humanly possible to listen to such a buzzing. She never stops. I feel as if I had been two hours in a mill-wheel.

LÉONARD.
Miserable woman! Don't let her come down. Alizon! Gilles! Shut her up!

ADAM.

My good sir!

MLLE DE LA G.

Oh, sir, can you be so hard-hearted as to keep the poor lady shut up?

CATHERINE.

What a numerous and delightful company. Your servant, gentlemen.   [*She curtseys.*

SIMON.

And now, tell me, Madame, are you not satisfied with us? and have we not thoroughly loosed your tongue?

CATHERINE.

You did it very well, gentlemen, and I am much obliged to you. Just at first I could not articulate a good many words. But now I have considerable facility of speech. I use it with moderation, for a talkative woman is a domestic scourge. Gentlemen, I should be inconsolable if you had reason to suspect me of loquacity or if you thought an itch for speaking had hold of me. Therefore, I ask your leave to put myself right at once in my husband's sight, for he, prejudiced on I know not what grounds against me, has conceived that my conversation distracted him in a vexatious manner when he was propounding a judgment . . . a judgment in favour of a young orphan girl, whose father and mother were cut off in the flower of her youth. But no matter. I was sitting by him and hardly addressed a word to him, so to say. All I did was to sit there. Can a husband complain of that? Can he complain of a wife's sitting near him and seeking his company, as she ought to? (*To her husband.*) The more I think about it the less I understand your impatience. What was the cause of it? Don't say again that it was my chatter. The excuse cannot be sustained. My friend, you must have some grievance against me that I am ignorant of, and I beg you to tell me it. You owe me an explanation, and when I know what has vexed you I will see to it that you are spared in future the annoyance you have brought to my knowledge. For I am anxious to shield you from every occasion of discontent. My mother used to say: "Between husband and wife there should be no secrets." And she was right. A husband or a wife has, at times, as a result of not confiding the one in the other, drawn down on the household or on themselves the most terrible calamities. That is what happened to the wife of the President of Beaupréau. To give her husband an agreeable surprise she shut up a little sucking-pig in a box in her room. The husband heard it squeal, and thinking it was a lover, drew his sword and thrust it through his wife's heart before he heard the unhappy woman's explanations. When he opened the box, judge of his surprise and his despair. That is why there should never be anything hole and corner, even when well meant. You can say what you like before these gentlemen. I have done no wrong, and whatever you may say my innocence will only show the more clearly.

Léonard
(*who, for some moments, has been vainly trying, by his signs and exclamations, to stop* CATHERINE's *flow of words, and who has already given signs of extreme impatience*).
The powder! The powder! Master Simon Colline, your powder—your white powder, for pity's sake!

Simon.
· Never, indeed, was deafening powder more necessary. Be good enough to sit down, worshipful sir. Master Séraphin Dulaurier will blow the deafening powder into your ears.

Séraphin.
With pleasure, sir.

Simon.
There—it is done.

Catherine (*to* Maître Adam Fumée).
Make my husband listen to reason, Master Lawyer. Tell him he must hear what I have to say—that a wife must not be condemned unheard—tell him that one does not throw bags at a woman's

head—for he threw bags at my head—without being driven to do it by some violent impulse, mental or emotional. But no! I will speak to him myself. (*To* Léonard.) Answer me, my friend, have I failed you in any way? Am I a wicked woman? Am I a bad wife? I have done my duty faithfully. I will go so far as to say that I have loved . . .

Léonard
(*his countenance expresses beatitude, and he twiddles his thumbs tranquilly*).
How delicious! I hear nothing now.

Catherine.
Listen to me, Léonard. I love you tenderly. I will open my heart to you. I am not one of these light and frivolous women a mere nothing can cast down and a mere nothing console, and who are amused with trifles. I feel the need of friendship. I was born so. When I was no more than seven I had a little dog, a little yellow dog . . . You are not listening to me . . .

Simon.
Madame, he cannot listen to you or to anyone else. He no longer hears.

Catherine.
What do you mean, he no longer hears?

SIMON.
He can no longer hear because of a drug he has taken . . .

SÉRAPHIN.
. . . Which has resulted for him in a calm and cheerful deafness.

CATHERINE.
I will make him hear me.

SIMON.
You can do nothing of the sort, Madame, it is impossible.

CATHERINE.
You shall see. (*To her husband.*) My friend, my dearest, my love, my heart, my better half . . . you don't hear. (*She shakes him.*) Olibrius, Herod, Bluebeard, cuckold . . .

LÉONARD.
I hear her no longer through my ears. But I hear her only too plainly in my arms, shoulders, and backbone.

SIMON.
She is going mad.

LÉONARD.

Whither can I flee? She has bitten me! I feel that I am becoming as mad as she!

[*The blind man is heard without. He enters the hall singing:*

>   Riverward wend you,
>   Arm clipped in arm,
>   Tra-la-lal-la,
>   Mill-maiden, send you
>   Take no alarm!
>   Trip you and bend you,
>   Flaunting each charm,
>   Tra-la-lal-la,
>   Mill-maiden, send you
>   Come not to harm!

[CATHERINE *and* LÉONARD, *dancing and singing, proceed to bite all the company who, in turn, become mad, dance and sing furiously, and only halt at length to allow* MONSIEUR LÉONARD BOTAL *to say:*

Ladies and gentlemen, be lenient to the author's shortcomings.

FINIS.

CHARACTERS.

MADAME DE SESCOURT (GERMAINE)
MADAME LAVERNE (CÉCILE)
NALÈGE
JACQUES CHAMBRY
FRANÇOIS

A drawing-room in Paris, 1895.

COME WHAT MAY

A COMEDY IN ONE ACT

Scene I.

Germaine, *then* Cécile.

Germaine (*alone, writing*).

Acroclinium, rose, twelve packets ; double acroclinium, white, twenty-four packets. Alpine plants are all small. And if I am to choose the species you must tell me whether they will have a north or south aspect . . .

Cécile (*coming in*).

Good morning, Germaine. I am fortunate. You are not yet flown.

Germaine.

Good morning, Cécile. You have something to tell me ?

Cécile.

No, nothing . . . everything. . . . Never mind Finish your letter.

GERMAINE.

I have but a couple more lines to write. (*Writes.*) Californian Eschscholtzia, mandarin, rose . . .

CÉCILE.

Good heavens! whatever is that?

GERMAINE (*writing*).

A flower, my dear girl, a pretty little white flower touched with rose. (*Writing.*) Heliotropium, Browalle Czerwiakowskii.

CÉCILE.

Goodness! In what language do you conduct your correspondence?

GERMAINE.

In the language of seedsmen. I am replying to Adalbert who wants me to choose him flowers for his garden. Each spring, for five years past, comes the same touching letter: " Dear Germaine, when my poor brother was alive you chose flowers for the parterres at Seuilly. Do so now that Seuilly is mine. You have so much taste." I cannot refuse him. And whatever I do, the parterres at Seuilly will be none the fairer for it.

CÉCILE.

Why?

GERMAINE (*closing her letter*).

I don't know. It is a gift. The Sescourts are unfortunate in all their undertakings. My husband had but a single passion—horses. His stable was always unlucky. Adalbert loves flowers. Flowers will not grow for him.

CÉCILE.

Do you think it is so?

GERMAINE.

I am sure of it.

CÉCILE.

But your husband was a much cleverer man than Adalbert.

GERMAINE.

Do you say that to flatter me, or because you think it?

CÉCILE.

Oh, I know that he was not the last word in husbands. He was not incomparable. You deserved a better. But I have ideas on the subject. A woman should not be so well married. On the contrary, a good marriage becomes an inconvenience in the end. Yes, I assure you . . . it prevents things. I, for instance, have a husband . . .

GERMAINE.

A charming one! Your husband is charming.

CÉCILE.

Charming! Well, it has put a stop to everything. I tell myself at times that there is some good in a bad match. It leaves an opening, it leaves possibilities, and one can hope at large. A delicious state! . . .

GERMAINE.

You have some very unruly notions to-day, my dearest. Say at once, with Paul Chambry, that a woman marries only to get into circulation

[*Enter* NALÈGE.

SCENE II.

The same and NALÈGE.

NALÈGE (*to* MADAME DE SESCOURT).
Madame!
(*to* MADAME LAVERNE).
Dear Madame! [*He bows.*

CÉCILE.

Monsieur de Nalège! . . . I thought you were at home, in your woods.

NALÈGE.

I come from them, Madame. I came but yesterday.

CÉCILE.

Your first visit is for Madame de Sescourt. I

claim the second for myself. Come and see me when you leave here. You will find my husband, who grows every day more devoted to you, and soon will be unable to get on without you. Which, for once in a way, does not mean . . . I will leave you. I have visits to pay from which I may not dispense myself, for they are to people I do not know. Good-bye. Exchange confidences of the fairest, and, if you speak of me, say: " She is lovable." [*She goes out.*

Scene III.

Germaine *and* Nalège.

Germaine.
True enough, she is lovable.

Nalège.
Very.

Germaine.
Isn't she? And men don't seem to see it. She says to me time and again: " I am not plainer than others, nor sillier. And yet—you may not believe it—no one makes love to me."

Nalège.
And to you they do it all day long?

GERMAINE.
Pooh!

NALÈGE.
All day long.

GERMAINE.
No. From five to seven.

NALÈGE.
And it amuses you to hear all their insipidities, their nonsense. It flatters you to receive the compliments of imbeciles who do not mean a single word they say.

GERMAINE.
Monsieur de Nalège, what have you been doing with yourself this winter?

NALÈGE.
I, Madame? I have lived alone in my woods, with my dog, my pipe, and my gun. I have passed whole days without seeing a human countenance. Two days ago I slept in a charcoal-burner's empty hut. I had lost myself in my own forests on a grand stormy night.

GERMAINE.
Just so! Such existence has left on you a trace of the wilds.

NALÈGE.

Ah! You find me rough because I tell you that you are fond of empty compliments.

GERMAINE.

Not at all.

NALÈGE.

. . . and because I suspect you of being entertained by fine words which hold but little meaning. Do you believe, Madame, that you are not to be caught as others are by phrases and grimaces? Do you believe that it is so easy to detect true feeling, and to see to the depths of the heart?

GERMAINE.

I believe that men can see nothing in that regard, even the cleverest. A silly woman can make them believe anything she wishes. Vanity blinds them. And women are not taken in by grimaces. They can very well distinguish under compliments the feelings that inspire them.

NALÈGE.

You are sure of that?

GERMAINE.

Certainly I am. We see at once with whom we have to do.

NALÈGE.

Yes, you think, you women, that you have a mysterious gift, that you hold the divining-rod which strains towards the hidden point of love. You believe that you can tell, among all others, the one who loves you the most and the best. Women are never mistaken. They say so, and they believe it until long experience has disabused them. I knew in her old age an Italian princess, a former beauty in Milan—and in Paris, too—in the days when Frenchmen wore nankeen trousers and sang Béranger's songs. In her declining days she would tell her tales to a grand-nephew of hers. And one day she began in these words: "At that time I was perfectly beautiful." The young man clicked his tongue and looked at his grand-aunt, as much as to say: "and you profited by it!" Thereupon the princess replied, with a sigh: "Well, then, if you will have it, nephew mine, I have been abominably robbed in my time." The fact is that in these matters the women and the men proceed . . . I do not say by touch, for that obviously would not be such a bad way of going about it—I will not say as at blind-man's buff, for at that people scream danger at you, but crossways through all sorts of phantasmagoria and devilments, like Don Quixote when he bestrode the good steed Chevillard to pursue the Infanta.

Germaine.

Extraordinary person that you are! You issue from your charcoal-burner's hut to persuade me, by means of an Italian princess and Don Quixote, that a woman cannot see when someone has a feeling—a liking—for her.

Nalège.

Even so. Sincere feeling, profound passion—a woman can pass them by without seeing them.

Germaine.

Oh, do not let us talk of passion. We have no notion on the subject. One does not know passion by sight—one has never seen it——

Nalège.

Never?

Germaine.

Never. Passion is like a thunderstorm—it never hits the mark. Once at Grand' Combe I was caught in a thunderstorm. I took refuge from it. The sky seemed on fire, the thunder never ceased its rumbling. The lightning split a poplar from crown to base a hundred yards from me. I was none the worse. Passion is like the thunderbolt—it is terrible, but it falls wide. A sentiment, on the other hand ... a liking ... a woman may inspire them—well and good—and she is aware of it.

NALÈGE.
Madame, I will give you methodical proof to the contrary. I am a man of method. I have a scientific mind. I have applied these faculties to agriculture. The results were disastrous. But a rational method must be judged in itself and not by effects for which it is not altogether responsible. I am going to prove to you, in the most rigorous manner, that, generally, if a woman perceives that one has a liking for her, it is because that sentiment is not very pronounced, and that the stronger it is the less she will recognize it.

GERMAINE.
Proceed with your demonstration.

NALÈGE.
Must we first define this ... liking ... of which we speak?

GERMAINE.
That would not help us.

NALÈGE.
No, Madame, it would not be without use. But it would, perhaps, border on impropriety.

Germaine.
Impropriety ? Why, what do you mean ?

Nalège.
I think a precise definition might offend your delicacy. And what I say should not cause you surprise for, in fact, when a man is sitting thus near a lady, as I am near you, and says to himself in his heart as he looks at her—thus, as I am looking at you: "Madame So-and-so is delightful," this reflection holds . . . I hope it may not shock you ?

Germaine.
Not at all.

Nalège.
The reflection has in it the germ of an idea at the same time natural, physical, psychological, the presentation of which in all its strength and simplicity is utterly opposed to established manners. The mere reflection that "Madame So-and-so is delightful" denotes when it crosses the mind the birth of a sequence of vivid pictures, of curious feelings, and violent desires which succeed one another, multiply themselves, rush to the front, and know no pause till—which know no pause, Madame . . .

Germaine.
You trifle !

NALÈGE.

No, Madame, I do not trifle. I am but establishing the groundwork of my argument. It follows from what I have just set forth that the ordinary, average, everyday man who thinks, as he sees you, " She is charming," and who entertains the thought without ardour of sentiment, without power of reflection, without strength of soul or body, without even knowing what he thinks or whether he thinks at all, such an one may stay near you and be pleasing, endearing, ingratiating. He talks, smiles, has the will to please. He pleases. Whereas the unhappy man who, above all others, thinks that she is charming, but also feels the full force of that thought, he contains himself, conceals it, shuts it away. He is fearful lest it escape, in spite of him, in untimely turbulence, and he is uneasy. He is mute and depressed. You think he is bored, and he bores you. You say : " Poor man, he becomes rather wearisome." And that because he is only too well aware of your grace and beauty, because he has received a mortal thrust, because he has conceived a strong and generous inclination towards you. Because, in a word, he is —as people used to say—very hard hit.

GERMAINE.

He is somewhat absurd, your good man.

Nalège.

Certainly. He is conscious of the disproportion existing between the ideas he entertains and those he must express. He feels himself ridiculous. He becomes so. It is an absurd incongruity, a burlesque breach of manners, to think of a lady too clearly in terms of a woman. The thought may border on the tragi-comic.

Germaine.

And then——

Nalège.

Then, instead of making pretty speeches and venturing oneself adroitly, one shows oneself downcast and timid. Even if one is not so by nature, one becomes so. One gives up all attempt at saying what may only be said by overweakening its expression. One falls into a dull despondency, into a stupidity that weighs one down . . . [*A silence.*

Germaine.

. . . from which one issues no more ?

Nalège.

From which one issues at the first charming note of the beloved voice. One gathers oneself together, one starts again . . . and if one happens to be a rustic and a ruminant, a solitary who has wandered dreaming in the woods with his gun, his book, and his dog, one spins wide theories, lays down systems, holds forth on the subject of love. One takes up again the thread of long demonstrations. One argues. It is a foolish business to argue in the presence of a pretty woman, but one argues. One grows dogged, and follows one line of argument with obstinacy and contentiousness . . . or perhaps . . .

GERMAINE.

Or perhaps . . . ?

NALÈGE.

Or perhaps one has a brusque change of mood. One becomes gay, trifling, flippant, indulges in pleasantry. One springs up and sits down again, looks about, interests oneself in odds and ends, says: "Here's a pretty miniature on this box." (*He picks up a box from the table.*) Who is this lady in powder—do you know?

GERMAINE.

It is Mademoiselle Fel.

NALÈGE (*dryly*).

Ah . . . Mademoiselle Fel.

GERMAINE.

At least, I believe so. You may compare it with the pastel by Latour at St.-Quentin.

Nalège.

I will not fail to do so, Madame. Thank you for having given me an interesting occupation. I will give my leisure time to it.

Germaine.

Why do you employ that tone ? What is the matter ?

Nalège.

Nothing whatever. I proceed with my demonstration. I say, you look round, you make yourself pleasant—lumberingly pleasant—you gambol like an elephant, or perhaps . . . do you follow me ?

Germaine.

I am with you . . . go on.

Nalège.

You take an inward revenge. You decry with sincerity—oh, yes, sincerely . . . the too precious object. You look at it with the eye of a disdainful connoisseur. You say to yourself: "I see well enough . . . clear and pure colouring, light golden hair, pretty skin, neck and shoulders of harmonious line, rounded and supple figure." Well, after all—is it unique ? Is it rare ? One knows what it is. What folly to hanker after it, what folly to suffer for it !

Germaine.
Ah! does one indeed?

Nalège.
Yes, you say that, and you try to believe it. And then you pity your very self. You long for some happiness, some rest and tranquillity. You say to yourself: "Go—go and smoke your pipe in the woods, seek your horse and your dog, seek the open sky, idiot that you are. And you pick up your hat (*he takes his hat*) and say: "Good day, Madame." [*He leaves.*

Scene IV.

Germaine *alone. Later*, François.

Germaine.
He has gone. . . . Pleasant journey, Monsieur de Nalège. Au revoir . . . good-bye . . . good-bye . . . au revoir. Who knows? A little brusque, a little queer, Monsieur de Nalège. What can one expect? . . . A man who sleeps out in the woods in a storm, in a charcoal-burner's hut! Five o'clock. . . . A savage who, nevertheless . . . Ah! my letter to poor Adalbert! . . . (*She rings.*) Perhaps what Cécile says is true, that Adalbert is

more stupid than . . . his brother. But that is of no importance . . . oh ! . . . none . . . (*Enter* FRANÇOIS). That is for the post. . . . If anyone calls, I am not at home. (FRANÇOIS *gives her a card, which she reads.*) Jacques Chambry . . . Show him in.

SCENE V.

GERMAINE, JACQUES CHAMBRY.

GERMAINE.

It is quite by chance that you find me at home. Usually I do not return home so early.

CHAMBRY.

By chance ? Rather by good luck . . . such a pleasure.

GERMAINE.

And a somewhat rare pleasure, for you do not often indulge in it. For instance, yesterday, at the play, you did not come to see me in my box. You denied yourself that pleasure.

CHAMBRY.

I did not dare. . . . Positively did not dare.

In your box I perceived dragons, ogres, ogresses, dwarfs—it was terrifying.

GERMAINE.

What do you mean, dragons and ogres?

CHAMBRY.

A fairy's bodyguard; quite as it should be. But I shuddered. Behind you was counsel in the person of Billaine, rolling his great eyes; Colonel Herpin, weeping behind your back; and Baron Michiels, sleeping. He was the dwarf. He was quite appalling.

GERMAINE.

The play was charming. Did you not think so?

CHAMBRY.

Oh, yes. Boring—yes, very boring.

GERMAINE.

But no, I assure you—delightful, charming.

CHAMBRY.

Charming? Possibly. I only saw one act . . .

GERMAINE.

Come, come—you stayed in the beautiful Madame

Desenne's box all the time. There were no dwarfs, or ogres, or dragons in her box. There was only Desenne, who is deaf, and little Malcy, who is dumb. You were quite happy there.

CHAMBRY.

Very, Madame. I could see you all the time.

GERMAINE.

From afar.

CHAMBRY.

From afar, but in duplicate. I saw you full face and in profile at the same time. You were reflected in profile in the mirror of the stage-box—showing the nape of your neck. And it is not always that the nape of the neck is pretty. Nay, it is very rare. I have seen but five so far . . .

GERMAINE.

You are a collector?

CAMBRY.

In so far as I have a correct eye and know how to use it. Do not laugh. It isn't everyone who has the faculty. I know people who have loved a woman for months, years . . . three years . . . four years . . .

Germaine.
Four years . ?

Chambry.
If that frightens you, say eighteen months—two years . . . men who have adored a woman for years, who have loved her . . . in every way . . . and who do not even know if she is well made, or what are her good and what her second-rate points. They are not aware of these things, and they never will be. They lack the trained eye, and that is irreparable. On people like that exquisite things are lost. People whose eyes are unable to read a woman constitute the great majority. I can give you an example. You know Thouvenin, old Thouvenin of the Congo Railway. You know that he has lived for years with Mercédès, the dancer . . .

Germaine.
No—I know nothing whatever about it.

Chambry.
Anyhow, it is so. Well, one day last week I came across Thouvenin in a very well-known house. But not of your world. He was in the drawing-room, turning over an album filled with portraits of young ladies, whose only costumes were their ear-rings and their rings. I was looking over

his shoulder. All at once I caught sight of a slight, slender brunette, who possessing no veil but her fan was, with very proper feeling, hiding her eyes with it. I said to Thouvenin: "There is Mercédès." Staggered, he exclaimed: "Where?" "There, Monsieur Thouvenin, there in the book of specimens. "Impossible—what makes you think so?" "Everything." "Nothing that I can see. How do you expect one to recognize her?" And pray observe that Thouvenin is parting with 15,000 francs a month for the possession of charms that he fails to recognize when he can't see the tip of her nose. The moral of this story . . .

GERMAINE.

Oh—there is a moral?

CHAMBRY.

And you shall unravel it yourself.

GERMAINE.

I? I do not even know what you have been saying. I was not listening.

CHAMBRY.

Listen, at least, to the moral. . . . It is melancholy to have to tell oneself one is pretty; but there are few connoisseurs, very few.

Germaine.

So you have merely a vague idea of this play we saw ... together. That is a pity. It was interesting.

Chambry.

But I have already told you, I only looked at you. You will never know how charming you looked last night.

Germaine.

Describe me, then, describe me. I am certain that you do not even know the colour of my gown.

Chambry.

Your gown ... the colour ...? (*After a while.*) Blue.

Germaine.

What a pity that you were unable to see yourself as you replied " Blue "! You were like this: (*she imitates him*). Wandering eyes, puckered brow, arm outstretched, with fingers feeling in the air like a small boy drawing a number out of a bag.

Chambry.

Well?

Germaine.

Well, you have won.

Chambry.
And that blue gown suited you to perfection.

Germaine.
Oh, you thought so? As it happened, an old friend who was in my box said to me: " That dress does not suit you at all. You are a hundredfold prettier in pink than in blue." And I confess, Monsieur Chambry, I was touched and flattered by this remark because I believed it to be the truth, because I felt its sincerity and that it betokened a real desire to see me to my advantage.

Chambry.
It was the dwarf who told you that?

Germaine.
The dwarf?

Chambry.
Yes, Baron Michiels. He affects a rough outspokenness with you. He subjugates you by his calm assurance in judging your frocks. Well, he is colour-blind. He cannot tell red from green. One day in a sale room I found him in ecstasy over some cherries by Madeleine Lemaire. He thought they were plums. Just imagine, then, how this gnome must appreciate the rose of your cheek,

which melts so imperceptibly into the soft white of your throat . . .

GERMAINE.
Poor Monsieur Michiels! He is such a good friend. So devoted.

CHAMBRY.
Do not believe it. He is sulky, and evilly disposed, that is all. What advantage can you see in surrounding yourself with a bodyguard borrowed from the Law Courts, the Stock Exchange, and the Army, which watches over you with a vigilance at once fierce and grotesque? You are never to be found alone.

GERMAINE.
It appears to me that at this moment . . .

CHAMBRY.
Ah, once in a way—in your drawing-room, with doors. It is all doors, this room.

GERMAINE.
There are four. It is like every other drawing-room. Surely you do not imagine . . .

CHAMBRY.
Lord! yes—I do imagine . . .

GERMAINE.
I am ignorant of your ideas on furnishing. I like

airy rooms, bright, and with simple lines and plenty of space.

Chambry

(*rises, and examines first the things on a table, next in a glass-fronted cupboard, then on a side table*).

You have taste, you have a feeling for art, it is true. You may believe me. I understand the matter.

Germaine.

I do believe you.

Chambry.

You have some nice things. Those perfume burners are very pretty in their old setting . . . old china . . . old Sèvres, celadon . . . soft paste. . . (*He takes up a box from the table.*) This box, with a miniature on a ground of vernis Martin, striped like one's great-grandmother's frock, is pleasing to the eye and to the touch. I love knick-knacks that one may handle with pleasure, which love, themselves, to be caressed. This miniature is a portrait of a well-known woman. It is . . . wait a moment . . . I will tell you . . .

Germaine.

It is said to be Mademoiselle Fel.

Chambry.

And it is. She resembles Latour's pastel.

GERMAINE.
Oh, so you know Latour's pastel? Good!

CHAMBRY.
That surprises you because you only consort with savages. Do you like miniatures? Because if you like them I could show you some rather pretty ones at my house.

GERMAINE.
Yes, I like miniatures very much, but not to excess.

CHAMBRY.
And would one have to love them to excess to come and see some to-morrow between five and six at No. 18 Place Vendôme, ground floor, left-hand side, no stairs, just three steps?
[*He picks up a book from the table.*

GERMAINE.
Look what you are holding in your hand.

CHAMBRY.
I see . . . morocco binding . . . delicate tooling. Superb!

GERMAINE.
You will not be able to lay the blame upon me for having given it you. You have found it for your-

self. Who is it says, "One cannot avoid one's fate"? You have gone to meet yours. What you hold in your hand is the Album. Yes, monsieur, that morocco binding is its cover. I, like all the rest, have one. [*She offers him a pen.*

CHAMBRY (*turning over the leaves*).

I see, it is an autograph album. And, as such things go, it is not too bad. . . . Falguière, Paul Hervieu, Massenet . . . Henri Lavedan, Paul Bourget, Deschanel, Ludovic Halévy. . . . All the elect. Distinguished names crowd its vellum. Ah, —here and there one finds others less illustrious. I do not know whether I am mistaken, but it seems to me that names such as Janvier Dupont, Colonel Herpin, and Paul Floche, do not shine with dazzling effulgence. You mingle the illustrious and the obscure in your album.

GERMAINE.

That is all as it should be. And I will tell you why. Sometimes—oh, not often—a man of the world will write a pretty thing in this album—a celebrity, never! Oh, you may judge yourself, for look what Jules Lemaître, Pailleron, Sardou, Vanderem have written.

CHAMBRY

(*turning over the leaves and reading in an undertone*).

Yes. You are quite right. . . . Insignificant . . . feeble . . . nothing at all.

GERMAINE.

And what about Dumas? Read what Dumas has written. At the beginning . . . at the top of a page . . . there——

CHAMBRY (*reading aloud*).
"*At the beginning of winter we have the chimneys swept.*"   ALEXANDRE DUMAS fils.

CHAMBRY (*reading aloud*).
"*Love blossoms in our tears.*"   PAUL FLOCHE.

GERMAINE.

Now, that is pretty.

CHAMBRY.

Yes, it is pretty. And it recalls an impression one has experienced sometimes, something one has felt before. What is he, this Monsieur Paul Floche?

GERMAINE.

I do not quite know. I think he has something to do with wood pavements. (*Seeing* CHAMBRY *is about to close the album.*) Oh, your turn has come. You are not going to get off. Write . . .

CHAMBRY (*opening the album*).
What depresses me is not so much what is

written here, it is this white—all this blank space. The sight of it makes one think of all the inanities to come, of all the feeble, halting, abortive thoughts that the future may have in store (*he writes*), and which will find a home here.

GERMAINE.

Write!

CHAMBRY.

It is done, Madame. It is done.

GERMAINE.

What have you put? (*He holds out the album, and* GERMAINE *reads aloud.*) "*Love is a stream that mirrors Heaven.*" It is charming.

CHAMBRY.

And I believe it. Yes, I believe that did love not add colour to our life we should perish from despair and boredom. I am a dreamer, at heart a sentimentalist.

GERMAINE.

"*Love is a stream that mirrors Heaven,*" It is delicious. But water flows if the heavens remain. You are pledged to nothing.

CHAMBRY.

The stream unceasingly gives back the sky and

murmurs and flows unceasingly. The stars of heaven tremble in its waves.

GERMAINE.
But, tell me, does this stream flow from a spring?

CHAMBRY.
But . . .

GERMAINE.
Or does it not rather issue from a reservoir, from a very small reservoir whose key you hold, and which you lock up on a fine evening before going out walking?

CHAMBRY.
You are rash. You are to be blamed if you mock at love.

GERMAINE.
I am not mocking at love. At the worst, I am only mocking at your little stream.

CHAMBRY.
It is wrong of you. And more unfair than you imagine. If you only knew . . .

GERMAINE.
Ah, but you see, I don't know.

Chambry.

You believe me incapable of feeling—of tenderness?

Germaine.

I confess that I have no views on the subject.

Chambry.

Yes, yes. Madame, because I do not affect a blunt outspokenness, like Baron Michiels, because I do not roll great eyes, like old Billaine, because I do not weep on your shoulder silently during a whole evening, like the gallant Colonel Herpin—you imagine I am indifferent, that I am unable to appreciate you, that I fail to see that you are charming, exquisite, adorable.

Germaine.

I do not imagine anything, believe me, I beg of you.

Chambry.

You misjudge me: you do not believe in me. Shall I tell you why? Because in love you are all for the classic tradition, for the established forms, for the protocols. You would be made love to by method, you lean to lovers grave and correct. That is a perversity. They ruin a woman when they get her, people of that kind. Do not put yourself in their hands—it would be a crime.

GERMAINE.

Have you been to the Exhibition of Water Colours yet ? It is a very good show this year.

CHAMBRY.

Why do you not believe that I love you ? Because I have not told you so ? Well, sometimes the more one thinks the less one says.

GERMAINE.

Frankly, Monsieur Chambry, had you told me so I should believe it none the more.

CHAMBRY.

Why ?

GERMAINE.

Because as soon as you get to know a woman you say that sort of thing as naturally as another man tells you that it's raining or that it's a fine day. The thought has no importance for you. You have not given it a thought—you say it and you think no more about it. It is a mere civility.

CHAMBRY.

No—oh, no !

GERMAINE.

An incivility then, if you like.

CHAMBRY.

Nevertheless, it is true that I love you. And if I tell you so after the fashion you describe, it is certainly not to appear civil, not even to appear uncivil, however much I might wish to be so. It is quite simply because I am sincere, and because I *do* love you.

GERMAINE.

It is odd. . . . Yet one is bound to believe that there are women who are taken in by what you say—because if it did not come off now and then, you would probably have given it up. True enough, women are foolish at times.

CHAMBRY.

It is I who am foolish. Let us be foolish together. It is the best thing in the world. You have never been happy. You have never been loved. You do not know what it is. Do not waste your youth, your beauty. (*He kneels down and kisses her hand.*) Unbend, forgive, soften your heart. Do not become your own heart's enemy. Germaine, I beseech you . . . for my sake . . . for your own . . .

GERMAINE.

Get up. There is a ring at the bell. I hear someone coming.

CHAMBRY.
No, I will not get up. There is no one coming. No one must come. It would be ridiculous. Just like a theatrical scene. I shall remain at your feet. I shall keep your hand pressed to my lips until you believe me.

GERMAINE.
Oh, I believe—that I am not utterly distasteful to you. There! Get up.

SCENE VI.

The same. CÉCILE.

CÉCILE.
It is I once more, darling. How do you do, Monsieur Chambry?

CHAMBRY.
Madame, I am really enchanted . . .

CÉCILE.
I am sure you are. (*To* GERMAINE.) Is not Nalège here?

Germaine.

He left more than an hour ago—he went, indeed, in some haste.

Cécile.

It was to see me. But he will return, I told him to meet me here. He went off with my husband, who was to show him a horse on the way and drop him at your door. Why isn't he here by this time?

Chambry.

Oh, you will have to wait. When lovers of horses get their feet in the straw and their noses on a crupper, hours seem to them like seconds.

Cécile.

You do not know Monsieur de Nalège, his greatest delight is to be out with his gun and his book. But do not misjudge him, although very serious, he has a very pleasant side.

Chambry.

And plenty of wit. Unfortunately, it is like my Aunt Clemence's furniture. They say it is upholstered in admirable Beauvais, but no one has seen anything but the holland covers. Oh, were Nalège to take off his cover! What splendour would be revealed! But he will not take it off.

CÉCILE.
That is to say, he will not take it off for everyone. He is not commonplace.

CHAMBRY.
Anyway, he has an advantage for which I envy him. He pleases you. (*Then to* GERMAINE.) Dear lady . . .

GERMAINE.
Must you go ?

CHAMBRY (*in an undertone*).
I shall return. I must speak to you.

SCENE VII.

GERMAINE, CÉCILE.

CÉCILE.
Was he making love to you ?

GERMAINE.
A little. Does it show ?

CÉCILE.
A declaration of love shows when it " takes,"

like vaccination. It lends a slight rosiness to the skin.

Germaine.
How fond you are of talking nonsense.

Cécile.
But, dearest, it was easy to guess. He makes love to every woman. He has even made love to me. To me—whom men do not even look at! It is quite true, I have no success. And I am blessed if I know why . . . I am neither uglier, nor more stupid than others.

Germaine.
You are very nice to look at.

Cécile.
No, I am not nice looking. I am merely comfortable looking and normal—oh, normal. Do you remember when we attended Monsieur Blanchard's classes together? In one geographical atlas there were heads representing types of the human race: the black, the yellow race, and the white race. Well, the white race was a striking likeness of me. You wrote my name underneath.

Germaine.
And you complain! It was Venus!

CÉCILE.

Do you think so?

GERMAINE.

I am certain. The Medici Venus. Apollo was on her left—underneath a Red Skin. I can see them now.

CÉCILE.

Well then, you must believe that the Medici Venus is no longer in demand, save by Chambry. And the worst of it is that I am normal morally, as well as physically—normal to my very soul. Yes, indeed . . . You know underneath the white race was written in our atlas, "The women of this race are active, intelligent, courageous, and faithful." That is just what I am. I conform to type, neither more nor less. I am normal to absolute commonplace.

GERMAINE.

But you do not think me an exception—a monstrosity?

CÉCILE.

You, you possess charm, and I believe you are straight.

GERMAINE.

Thank you, Cécile.

CÉCILE.

Yes, I believe you are straight. I think so to begin with because it is pleasanter between friends —I must say it, and why shouldn't I believe it? Then, perhaps, it is true. I have no proof to the contrary.

GERMAINE.

Really?

CÉCILE.

And then, you are a widow, you are free. Liberty holds you back, perhaps. . . . I know quite well that you are not very sensible. But it is the sensible women who commit the greatest follies. For instance, Madame de Saint-Vincent, she was sensible, austere, classically beautiful, and with lofty sentiments. Well, no sooner did Chambry deign to insult her virtue than she fell swooning into his arms. Ever since she pursues him like a mad woman. Her children, her reputation, her husband's diplomatic career—she has sacrificed them all to this good-looking young scamp who laughs at her, as you may imagine.

GERMAINE.

It makes me nervous.

Cécile.

Oh, you know Chambry is a terrible undertaking for a woman. He is vain, he is a liar. I never give advice, even unasked—which, after all, is not quite as silly as to give it when one is asked! But were I to do so, how good my advice would be! I, dearest, hold no cards, so I see the game very well; while the most subtle players . . .

Germaine.

Do not give it, Cécile, do not give it. I should do the opposite, as people always do, and you would have a fearful responsibility. But do not be afraid. I shall commit no follies. There is one thing positive, though, and that is that I am bored with life. Well, seeing that I succeed in that so admirably by myself, it is superfluous to seek assistance. It is better to bore myself than to be bored, just as it is less irritating to do one's hair badly than to have it ill done by a lady's maid. I have no more illusions, my dear. Marriage made me quarrel with love. The men whom I meet have not yet induced me to patch it up. The sincere ones are deadly and the others—those who perchance afford us a little pleasure—make fun of us. Under these conditions it is hardly worth while complicating one's existence. I am neither tender-hearted nor generous, Cécile—give me your esteem—I have not enough heart to behave badly.

Cécile.

Agreed that you have not enough heart; but do not put too much trust in that. It is not absolutely necessary to be a saint to behave badly. Now, let us talk seriously. You are dining with me and we will go to the play. Nalège and my husband will come with us. Go and put on your hat. [FRANÇOIS *hands her a card.*

Germaine (*reading*).
Monsieur de Nalège.

Cécile.
Go and put on your hat, quickly. I will receive him.

Scene VIII.

Cécile, Nalège.

Cécile.
Madame de Sescourt begs you to wait for her a moment. She is just coming. Well—did you buy the horse that my husband took you to inspect?

Nalège.
Yes. Has Madame de Sescourt gone out to shed

the light of her presence elsewhere ? For in that case she will doubtless be long detained.

Cécile.
No, she is in her room, putting on her hat.

Nalège:
That will also take some time. But as it is one of the most important things she can very well do . . .

Cécile.
I fail to see the importance of it.

Nalège.
I see it very well. What stamps a woman, what gives her her rightful value, what makes her a power in the world which is only equalled by the possession of money, is her dress and her hat.

Cécile.
And her fine linen, Monsieur.

Nalège.
And her fine linen. You are quite right.

Céclie.
Monsieur de Nalège, you think women inferior

beings. Maybe you are not wrong in thinking so. But you are surely wrong to let them see it. It is not tactful.

Nalège.

Then you, Madame, want us to admire your sentiments as much as your hats ?

Cécile.

It is not a question of myself. Moreover, Monsieur de Nalège, do not be disagreeable to me. You have no excuse. You are not in love with me. And what's more, it would be unjust : I have just been praising you and defending you against Monsieur Chambry, who will have it that you keep on your cover.

Nalège.

My cover ?

Cécile.

Do not seek to understand . . . I said that you had a very cultured, exceedingly attractive, and not at all commonplace mind, and that you always had a book in your pocket. Is it so ?

Nalège.

It is true enough about the book.
    [*He pulls a little book out of his pocket.*

CÉCILE.
A serious author . . . a philosopher . . .

NALÈGE.
Or a poet. . . . This one is Ronsard.

CÉCILE (*taking the book from him*).
Show me. . . . Oh! how ancient he looks . . .

NALÈGE.
And I find him adorably young.

SCENE IX.

GERMAINE, NALÈGE, CÉCILE.

CÉCILE.
Here is Monsieur de Nalège, accompanied by Ronsard—a gentleman from Vendôme.

GERMAINE.
Ah, so you have returned, Monsieur de Nalège?

NALÈGE.
How could I help myself?

GERMAINE.

You are polite.

NALÈGE.

No, Madame, not polite enough. I was wrong. Forgive me.

CÉCILE (*turning over the pages of Ronsard*).

Monsieur de Nalège, you press flowers in the leaves of your books.

NALÈGE.

Yes, Madame. A bibliophile would find fault with me. But I read in the woods and I put in a flower to mark the pages I love.

GERMAINE.

Meanwhile, what happens to your dog and your gun?

NALÈGE.

They go to sleep.

CÉCILE.

There is a periwinkle at
  "*When you are old, at dusk, by candlelight.*"
Those lines are pretty, then?

NALÈGE.

The form is unpolished and the style old-fashioned. But I think them the most beautiful in the world. (*To* GERMAINE.) Do you not know them?

GERMAINE.

No.

NALÈGE.

What a pity.

CÉCILE.

And neither do I. I do not know them, and it is as great a pity. Even more so. For I have a great love for verse and understand it. But it is not a quality that shows. Whereas Germaine, because she inspires it, is thought to love it. . . . Oh, yes, she inspires it. Her album is full of poems dedicated to her. (*Turning over the leaves of the album.*) Listen:

"*Pourquoi l'azur de vos prunelles
Est-il soudain plein d'étincelles?*" [1]

And that is to be sung. There is music to the words. (*Turning the leaves.*)

"*A Madame de Sescourt.
Quand l'aubepine fleurie de tes bras
Étend ses rameaux las de blancheurs et de
  parfums.*" [2]

[1] Wherefore does the blue of your eyes
Suddenly become full of stars.

[2] When the bloom-laden hawthorn that is your arms
Stretches forth its branches languid with pallor and perfume.

NALÈGE.
Those are bold lines . . .

CÉCILE.
And a thought quite lately flowered.

"*L'amour est un ruisseau qui reflète le ciel.*"[1]

And this flower appears to-day, Germaine?

NALÈGE.
That is by Renan.

CÉCILE.
No, it is by Paul Chambry.

NALÈGE.
It is by Ernest Renan. He wrote those lines in every album indifferently.

CÉCILE.
Well, Paul Chambry has signed his name to them.

NALÈGE.
He is an impudent plagiarist, that's all!

GERMAINE.
No, if he had the thought he had the right to sign it.

[1] Love is a stream that mirrors Heaven.

CÉCILE.

Are you coming, Nalège? He did not want to come, and now he does not want to go. I have no time to wait for you. I must go and dress. . . . Germaine, dear, do not make us dine too late. The play begins at eight o'clock—try to get there not later than nine.

GERMAINE.

I do not remember ever having seen the opening of a play.

CÉCILE.

Neither do I! [*She goes out.*

SCENE X.

NALÈGE, GERMAINE.

GERMAINE.

What, Monsieur de Nalège, you let her go alone?

NALÈGE.

Only one word, Madame. A moment ago you thought me brusque, odd, and unbearable . . .

GERMAINE.

No, I failed to find such a quantity of attributes

in you—I merely thought you a little put out. That was owing, no doubt, to what we were talking about. You chose an unfortunate subject. Next time you must try another, that's all. There is no lack of others.

Nalège.

No lack of subjects of conversation between a French woman and a French man ? No, Madame, there is but one, but there can be infinite variations on it. In future, if you will allow me, I will treat it in an entirely different manner, and I shall be pleasing, amiable, and almost attractive.

Germaine.

I was going to suggest it.

Nalège.

Would you like it at once ?

Germaine.

Be quick, then. I can give you three minutes. My maid is waiting for me.

Nalège.

That is very little, so it must be an abridged edition, a summary. But the essentials shall be there, and I believe that you will be satisfied.

(*With a fictitious ardour and a pretence of gallantry.*)
So, Madame, I love but you. You alone fill my thoughts and trouble my mind. When I appear to linger near another, it is an excuse to look at you from afar, discreetly, without annoying you. I wait until the swarm which buzzes around you disperses. I want you to myself, to myself alone. I despair at having to dispute my right to you with so many others. Yet, nevertheless, you ought to know that I am the only one who admires you and understands you. You are the most beautiful, you alone are really beautiful. You embody the ideal formed in my dreams. You believe me to be frivolous, light, in love with every woman. I love only you. I love and admire you.

[*He makes a pretence of putting his arm round her waist.*

Germaine.
Monsieur de Nalège, the three minutes are over.

Nalège.
Yes, but I have had time to give you pleasure.

Germaine.
To give me pleasure is saying a great deal. But I confess I find you far more agreeable than you were recently.

NALÈGE.

Quite so. You find me agreeable because I talked to you as do those who delight in your prettiness. I pleased you because round my words hung the scent of untruth. Madame, whatever you may say, women are only captivated by make-believe.

GERMAINE (*at the door*).

Julie, put out my white frock. (*To* NALÈGE.) Monsieur de Nalège, you no longer please me in the very least. You make me regret your former natural manner, your transparency, as painters say. Go, and allow me to dress—we are to dine together and spend the evening together—you ought to be satisfied.

NALÈGE.

No, Madame. [*He goes out.*

SCENE XI.

GERMAINE *alone*.

GERMAINE.

He has forgotten his book ... "*Les Amours de Pierre de Ronsard.*" Chambry certainly does not tell me anything absolutely fresh—nothing that has not been said before, and that will not be said again. But he brought a certain charm of manner to it and a certain note which is his own. As regards Nalège . . . neither are his rough ways particularly novel. And they are irritating. . . . "*Les Amours de Pierre de Ronsard.*" . . . True, he presses flowers between the pages of his poet. This pretty custom is quite touching. He is a good fellow, after all—Nalège. Here is the periwinkle marking the tenderest verses. (*Reads.*)

> "*Live on, believe me, do not wait the morrow,*
> *Gather the roses of your life to-day.*"

Perhaps he is right—Monsieur de Nalège's poet.

"*Gather the roses of your life to-day.*"

Scene XII.

Germaine, Chambry.

Germaine.
You!

Chambry.
I was on the look-out. I climbed upstairs again. How he must bore you, your rustic! . . . At last we are alone. I have so much to tell you.

GERMAINE.

You were watching ? . . . You climbed . . . Monsieur Chambry, do me the kindness to go at once. You enter like a thief. You look as if you had come out of a cupboard. It is ridiculous.

CHAMBRY.

No, it is not ridiculous. You mean to say it is unusual. You are right, it is not conventional. I am fully aware of it.

GERMAINE.

Merely ridiculous.

CHAMBRY.

Let us say, inadmissable. It is the drawback to our position.

GERMAINE.

What do you mean ?

CHAMBRY.

It is the drawback to our position. It is full of drawbacks. It cannot go on. It would be most imprudent. It is *beforehand* that one runs the risk of compromising a woman. It is *beforehand* that the tactless thing occurs. Yes. Afterwards there is an understanding, agreement, mutual warning. One acts with prudence, and one avoids danger.

To compromise a woman *afterwards* one must be a cad or the greatest fool ... or else a savage, like Nalège. There is the kind of man who, were some luckless woman to grant him favours, would bear it writ large in his eyes like the numbers on loto cards.

Germaine.

Monsieur Chambry, my maid is waiting for me. Go away.

Chambry.

To be imprudent *afterwards* is unforgivable. It ought not to happen. But *beforehand* the most gallant gentleman in the world cannot be sure of himself. I would not guarantee that we are not being talked about. It has to be gone through.

Germaine.

It is strange that I am not angrier. Confess that you yourself find it strange.

Chambry.

On the contrary, it is very natural, since you know that I love you.

Germaine.

I wish you good night, Monsieur Chambry.

CHAMBRY.
Where are we going?

GERMAINE.
I?... I am dining at Madame Laverne's.

CHAMBRY.
No, you are not going to dine at Madame Laverne's.

GERMAINE.
I am not going to dine at...? You are mad! Eight o'clock... Cécile... and Monsieur de Nalège, who are waiting for me...

CHAMBRY.
Ah, no—not that of all things.... You will not dine with Nalège. You will dine with me somewhere in an arbour in the country.

GERMAINE.
You grow very ridiculous

CHAMBRY (*handing her a pen*).
Write... "My dear Cécile, an awful headache..."

GERMAINE.

Monsieur Chambry, I am speaking seriously now. Go away!

CHAMBRY.

No—I shall not go. I shall not allow you to meet Nalège again. Germaine . . . stay . . . I love you.

GERMAINE.

Go away, I beseech you.

CHAMBRY.

I cannot leave you. It is true, I cannot. It is stronger than I am . . . Germaine, you will make me very unhappy. I am speaking sincerely. Really, you will make me very unhappy.

GERMAINE.

Unhappy? Why? Because of Nalège?

CHAMBRY.

Yes.

GERMAINE.

Oh, well, if it is because of Nalège, don't be unhappy. There is no need to be, I assure you.

CHAMBRY.

Quite true? You prefer me?

GERMAINE.
I prefer you. Are you pleased?

CHAMBRY.
Very pleased.

GERMAINE.
Well then . . . now—go.

CHAMBRY.
To-morrow—five o'clock. You will come for certain? Three steps. . . . I will change the carpet in your honour. [*He goes out.*

GERMAINE (*alone*).
Come what may!

CPSIA information can be obtained
at www.ICGtesting.com
Printed in the USA
LVHW081749050322
712715LV00011B/883